Richard Firth is a methodist minister/presbyter with a
of experience in a wide variety of situations: city centre,
overseas, inner city, commuter town, urban and rural areas,
and retiring to the seaside. He has always had a concern for
the integrity of the Christian message and clarity of exposition
and communication. This book is the culmination of a
lifetime's thinking about this important subject and
deliberation upon a wide reading of commentaries and
theological works to which he is indebted for their
stimulation. He trusts that readers will be encouraged in their
own thinking to arrive at truth meaningful for themselves. He
is a graduate of Leeds, Greenwich (USA) and Birmingham
Universities, and married with a grown up family.

To my wife, Joyce, fellow pilgrim on the journey of life and the quest for the truth.

Richard Firth

Re-Viewing the Resurrection

AUSTIN MACAULEY PUBLISHERS™

LONDON • CAMBRIDGE • NEW YORK • SHARJAH

A CIP catalogue record for this title is available from the British Library.

ISBN 9781035814558 (Paperback)
ISBN 9781035814565 (ePub e-book)

www.austinmacauley.com

First Published 2023
Austin Macauley Publishers Ltd®
1 Canada Square
Canary Wharf
London
E14 5AA

It is a pleasure to acknowledge the help, advice and encouragement in writing this book of a good friend, Brian W.J.G. Wilson, a classical Greek scholar and retired head teacher, The Revd Dr Ian Duffield, emeritus director of research at the Urban Theology Union Sheffield, and Joyce, my dear wife and fellow pilgrim. My gratitude to them cannot be overstated, as I have sought to explore the resurrection of Jesus Christ and to understand the event and its significance for our times.

Richard Firth,
Tynemouth,
May 2023.

Table of Contents

Preface

The title of this book, I trust, speaks for itself. The Resurrection is an important subject and an integral element of traditional Christian doctrine. That is why we need to get as near to the truth as possible. Hopefully, what follows is a stage on the way to achieving this. We shall be reviewing the evidence for Jesus' resurrection, seeking to get into and behind the texts of the four Gospels, and the minds of those who were there or who wrote about it. It may well be that we shall then re-view the events of that 'third day' in a new light.

Commentaries on the texts, by and large, tend to treat the story of the resurrection literally and historically and follow the limitations of the methods of biblical criticism. A perusal of the range of commentaries in the Dewey no. 232 section of my local theological resource library reveals that almost without exception, the resurrection is treated as a real event which happened within history. It is difficult to understand why some of them do not question this interpretation, especially in the light of our scientific knowledge, psychological experience and methods of historical investigation. There is a need, also, to interpret the appearance stories in an experiential way.

The resurrection has traditionally been regarded as an

essential building block in the Christian message along with the incarnation, the passion and the crucifixion of Jesus. But are these part of the original 'good news' as proclaimed by Jesus Himself? We hope to reach more than a tentative conclusion to this question.

Whatever is in the hearts and minds of Christian people at Easter time, however literally or otherwise they regard the stories in the Gospels, this book will not necessarily change their perceptions, but it may help some who search for credibility because so often, these days, insofar as the Church is concerned, belonging to it means tolerating hosts of inadequacies, both in belief and behaviour. So reader, may this book help you in that elusive search for the truth in which all faithful disciples of Jesus are engaged.

It may be asked, "Why does it matter?" I believe that there is a need for credibility, especially as the resurrection is claimed to be the foundation of the Christian Faith and the origin of the Church. The resurrection may well be amongst those 'ten impossible things' we are asked to believe before breakfast!

Richard Firth
May 2023

Chapter 1
Considering Mark's End

Jean de la Fontaine (1621–1695) once said, "In all matters, one must consider the end." With regard to the resurrection of Jesus, we need a fresh and realistic look at the end of St Mark's Gospel, chapter 16, verses 1 to 8, with the following assumptions in mind, mainly based on accepted traditions:

- That Mark's Gospel was written c65AD in Rome
- That it was mainly based on the recollections of Peter according to Bishop Papias c130AD
- That Peter was martyred (by inverted crucifixion) in c64AD during Nero's persecution
- That Mark was martyred in Alexandria c68AD for his opposition to paganism
- That the abrupt ending of Mark's Gospel at 16.8 requires an explanation.

In addition, three other assumptions based upon present knowledge and experience:

- That it was scientifically impossible for the dead

Jesus to be brought back to life

- That God is not interventionist and does not circumvent His own natural laws as to do this would be to contradict Himself.
- That the theology of resurrection needs to be expressed in other than that of literal and physical terms.

The Ending of Mark's Gospel

The abrupt ending of Mark's Gospel has been the subject of much conjecture, and the use of gallons of ink in the writings of scholars over the centuries whose main alternatives as to the reason why are as follows[1]:

1. Mark intended to end the Gospel with chapter 16.1–8.
2. His original ending has been lost due to the mutilation of the scroll or the codex upon which the Gospel was written.
3. Mark was prevented by some circumstance or other from completing his Gospel.

Credence is usually given to alternatives 2 and 3 by the fact that the Gospel ends with *'gar'*, and that this is an ungrammatical way to end a sentence in Greek. The closing sentence of the Gospel thus reads: "for they were afraid" (*ephobounto gar*). However, there is evidence[2] from Greek

---

1 See Cry N.C. The Mutilation of mark's Gospel. Abingdon. 2003
2 Horst P...W. Van der. Can a Book End with Gar? JTS 23 1973.
P123.

literature to demonstrate that such an ending to a sentence, although unusual, is by no means uncommon, and so Mark could have ended his Gospel in this way. This writer affirms the opinion that the Gospel, as we have it, is the one that Mark intended for circulation in the early Church, but without the later addition of verses 9–20.

Also the importance of Mark 16.1–8, as a primary and primitive witness to the events of Easter Day itself is often overshadowed by the assertion that 1 Corinthians 15.3–5 is a prior source.[3] However, this is not necessarily so if Mark is based on Peter's oral tradition which would predate this. The one is not any less reliable than the other, especially as Paul's information was also second hand.

Again, with regard to Mark 16.1–8, the ambience of these verses is one of anguish, bewilderment and fear because of the sense of loss felt by the people involved, and their deep apprehension that, because of their association with Jesus, they would be the next to be arrested and put to death. The chief difficulty is that verses 6 and 7 do not seem to fit with this ambience as they do appear to introduce a note of triumphalism, affirmation and confidence, as traditionally interpreted. Why should this be so?

We need to bear in mind that the original Greek text was written as a continuous whole, without spaces or punctuation, which could be inserted at different places in transmission or translation. Moreover, it is suggested that under pressure of circumstances, perhaps Peter's imminent martyrdom, Mark did not write as fluently as he could have done, and that these

---

[3] *Scholarly consensus dates the Corinthian letters cAD 53–57 written from Ephesus*

last sentences of his Gospel were hurried jottings, and that there was a failure in coherence, although the ambience was intended to be the same throughout. The main issue concerns verses 5 to 7 but it will be useful to comment upon the whole passage, almost word for word, in order to arrive at a fresh interpretation, using imagination also as a tool of understanding. We shall use a translation, widely regarded as one of the most accurate there is, and resort to the original Greek at the crucial phrases.

Mark chapter 16 verses 1 to 8 (REB 1992)

Verse 1: When the Sabbath was over, Mary of Magdala, Mary the mother of James and Salome brought aromatic oils intending to go and anoint him.

The four Gospels record that Joseph and Nicodemus, with Pilate's permission, had hurriedly and perfunctorily placed the body of Jesus, with some initial form of anointing, in Joseph's tomb, and, with little opportunity for last rites and farewells from other disciples, friends and possibly family members.

(See Mark 15.42–47; Matthew 27.57–61; Luke 23.50–56; John 19.38–42)

The three women were evidently desirous of performing the due rituals in a more thorough manner.

Verse 2: And very early on the first day of the week just after sunrise, they came to the tomb.

The women had gone to the tomb as soon as it was

practically possible. Very likely, as they were grief-stricken, they had probably spent sleepless nights.

Verse 3: They were wondering among themselves who would roll away the stone for them from the entrance to the tomb...

In conversation, the women expressed the question which was uppermost in their minds. Their expectation was that the huge, heavy stone placed over the doorway of the tomb, as a security measure to retain the body of Jesus, would still be in place.

Verse 4: ...when they looked up and saw the stone, huge as it was, had been rolled back already.

Rather than using an earthquake or a divine agency (an angel?) to explain the rolling away of the stone, it is more realistic to believe that it was done by several human hands, most probably by a band of soldiers, as was rumoured, who had been instructed to remove the corpse from the tomb to suppress tales of a 'resurrection' or the veneration of the body, which would encourage anger or even an uprising among the people, with whom Jesus was a popular figure (Matthew 28.11–15).

Verse 5: They went into the tomb, where they saw a young man sitting on the right-hand side wearing a white robe, and they were dumfounded.

We may imagine the women hesitatingly entering the

tomb, being surprised to see the young man in a white robe sitting there on the ledge of the stone tomb which was empty. There is the possibility that the young man is Mark, providing his signature to the Gospel. (See also ch.14.51–52). He had been following the proceedings of the past few days very closely, so closely in fact that he was nearly arrested and only escaped the clutches of the authorities by slipping out of his robe as he was being apprehended. Upon recovering his garment later, or finding alternative dress, he continued to observe matters as closely as he could, and, on the morning after the Sabbath, he was the first to investigate the site of Jesus' entombment, finding the stone to be rolled away and the grave to be empty. It was then that the women arrived to find him sitting on the right-hand side of the tomb wondering what has happened.

Although there is no mention of an 'angel' here in Mark's Gospel, there is in Matthew (28.5–7) and Luke has, "two men in bright shining clothes" (24.4–7). Not a few commentators, therefore, take Mark's, "young man wearing a white robe" to be 'angelic', or a 'messenger of God', which is the meaning of *'angelos'*. We would prefer the more realistic interpretation that the young man, Mark, is indeed, in a sense, a messenger, but with the surprising news that the body of Jesus was gone. The women themselves are equally as surprised to see him sitting there all puzzled and bewildered at what has happened for he would have no knowledge, whatsoever, at what had transpired because he had turned up at the tomb expecting to find it intact.

Verse 6: But he said to them, "Do not be alarmed, you are looking for Jesus of Nazareth, who was crucified. He has been raised; He is not here, Look there is the place where they laid him."

The young man, whom we have presumed to be Mark, reassures the women, "It's only me." (Don't be alarmed!) He was probably known to them quite well as a member of the wider group of disciples and friends of Jesus, and, possibly, according to one tradition, as the son or relative of the owner of the upper room.

He states the obvious that Jesus, the one from Nazareth, as opposed to many other Jesus around at the time, for it was a common name; he is the one from Nazareth, again, a phrase related to his origins and identity; the one who was crucified, dead and buried, he is not here in this tomb. His body is gone. The visible evidence consists of an absent body.

"He has been raised." There is no mention of who or what has done the raising, whether it is that of a full-blown resuscitation or the lifting up and removal of the body to be taken away and dumped. It is commonly assumed by scholars, commentators and readers that Jesus was raised by God, miraculously by a divine intervention, but there is no evidence that this was the case although, admittedly, the text does allow such an interpretation.

But here is the crux of the matter, what does this phrase mean?

The Greek is *'egerthe'*. The tense is passive. The body is an entity that has been acted upon. It has had something done to it. Is the explanation a supernatural one or a natural one?

The meaning of the verb *'egeiro'* as to 'raise from the

dead' is only found in the Gospels and St Paul and not in other literature where it usually means 'to wake someone up' (active) or of 'being woken up' (passive) with no connotation of an awakening from death. However, there is no reason to believe that here in Mark's Gospel it means anything other than that the body was lifted up and carried away by unspecified persons rather than being awakened (from sleep or from death) in the sense of a restoration to life at the time (c30AD) with the possibility that after another 35 years or so of developing tradition ideas of a physical resurrection became associated with it.

So could 'He has been raised' be instead 'Has he been raised?' that is, a rhetorical question, in view of a body's absence.

'Has he been raised?' that is, physically raised up and removed by those, possibly soldiers, who have, on instruction, broken into the tomb, removed the body and taken it to the rubbish dump outside the city of Jerusalem, for burning, as was the custom for all crucified victims. In Matthew, this is mentioned as a rumour but by then, at the time of his writing, a physical resurrection had become an acceptable idea. It is possible that the Greek does allow this interpretation.

In view of the fact that one of our basic assumptions is scientific, in that the dead are never normally restored to life, such an explanation is quite reasonable, given the evidence we have and the circumstances at the time. It is only in recent times that on occasion the clinically dead may be resuscitated by the marvels of modern medical technology, but to die again in due course.

We reiterate here the belief that these last few verses of his Gospel were written in a hurry by Mark, that they were hastily jotted down under the pressure of Peter's pending execution. The use of such sanctified speculation is entirely justified, being no more and less valid than other opinions, especially that of a physical resurrection. It may be argued that this is counter to the weight of Church tradition but such is never itself necessarily sacrosanct in light of reason and experience.

Verse 7a: But go and say to his disciples and Peter… These words could not mean anything other than that the women were requested to pass on the news that the tomb was empty and nothing more, thus making sure that Peter, as 'leader' of the disciples, knows what has transpired. In any case, Peter, according to Luke 24.12 and John 20.3 turned up later to visit the site, presumably as a result of being informed that the body of Jesus was gone.

Verse 7b: …he is going ahead of you into Galilee … there you will see him … as he told you.

We note that the REB translation omits '*hoti*' after 'Peter' ('*hoti*' meaning 'that', indicating reported speech) presumably because it is regarded as a later editorial insert, which lends further weight to the view that these phrases may be taken to refer to Peter. Elsewhere, it is recorded that Peter and other disciples intended to return to their occupations as fishermen in Galilee (John 21.3). If this is the case, it is not known exactly when they did this.

The verse does not, of necessity, refer to a physical appearance of the risen Jesus who would meet them all in Galilee once again after some kind of rapid transit to the north! Even Eduard Schweizer, a traditional and literal commentator with regard to the resurrection, nevertheless says 'It is very unlikely that verse 7 contains a genuine but unfulfilled saying of Jesus which anticipated that as the resurrected One he would go to Galilee leading a band of disciples'[4]

Verse 8: Then they went out and ran away from the tomb, trembling with amazement. They said nothing to anyone, for they were afraid.

This verse completes the atmosphere of bewilderment, grief, alarm and fear, which has gripped the women. The use of the word 'amazement' here in the REB translation is perhaps inappropriate. It reflects a preconceived belief in a factual resurrection. Other translations have such words as 'distressed', 'terrified', 'bewildered', 'afraid', etc. The NEB has it that they were 'beside themselves with terror'.

The women were not exactly ecstatic at the situation, which they would have been if the young man had given them news of Christ's resurrection. His words, therefore, must have been rhetorical, not factual. How could they have been since he himself had witnessed nothing but an empty tomb which only infers that some person, or persons, have removed the body?

Some commentators believe that the Gospel was unfinished and that Mark intended to include one story, at least, of a resurrection appearance. That he did not do so 35+

---

[4] Schweizer E. *The Good News According to Mark.* SPCK. 1971. p365.

years after the event is of the utmost significance. The other Gospels, Matthew and Luke 50+ years later, and John 60+ years later, with their stories of resurrection appearances, therefore, display evidence, in Chinese whispers fashion, of the development of a tradition in which remembered incidents in the life of Jesus are transposed into post-death grief experiences in order to support views of resurrection to countermand Roman and Greek mythologies of dying and rising gods. There was a need to affirm that 'Jesus is Lord' as opposed to Caesar.

There could be another reason why Mark includes no stories of resurrection appearances and why his Gospel ends on a note of bewilderment, which is that he was sceptical about them, believing that Jesus' death was in fact the end.

He reports the finding of the empty tomb as an incontrovertible fact, and just leaves it there with nothing more to add.

Verses 9–20: This later ending was known about cAD140 but not as part of the Gospel until mentioned as such by Irenaus cAD180. As Eduard Schweizer notes, there are brief allusions in the passage to incidents in the other Gospels and the Acts of which the unknown compiler of vs.9–20 may have been aware. They could seem to be a credible conclusion although 17–18 are rather fanciful, referring to certain charismatic gifts which Paul (1 Cor. 13.1–3) regarded as unimportant, because for him the most significant gift of the Spirit was love... Verses 19–20 mention the resultant Ascension. If anything, these added verses are an indication that the other Gospels may have used imported material too. As mentioned elsewhere, the general tenor is out of kilter with what we believe usually happens in reality, what is normal and what matches with life experience.

Further Reflections:

There is no harm in any speculation so long as it is based on the evidence we have and fits in with our knowledge of normality. Our sanctified guesses should be regarded as no better and no worse than the contents of the last chapters of Matthew, Luke and John relating to the stories of the so-called resurrection 'appearances'. That such stories were included in the scriptures does lend them a certain authority but they are to be taken no more and no less literally than other stories in the Gospels and in the Old Testament. The rigours of critical interpretation are required of them all.

Traditions record that Peter, in his martyrdom, experienced an inverted crucifixion so as not to die in the same way as Jesus and that this occurred in Rome in AD64 during the Neronic persecution. If so, and if Mark included in his Gospel the memories of Peter, as is believed, and if these were jotted down in his visits to Peter in prison, then there would be pressure to complete them asap.

Tradition again records the death of St Mark by hanging in Alexandria in AD68, following his resistance to pagan religion. Calculations that the Gospel, therefore, was written in about AD65 may probably be correct. The short last chapter is evidence that the work, most carefully written in chapters 1–15, was finished hurriedly recording the barest of facts. It is the view of this writer that such jottings became conflated into a single continuous text and that the overall ambience of 16.1–8 is of grief-stricken bewilderment and that any note of triumphalism attached to verses 6 and 7 is a misinterpretation because of the serious question we have concerning a literal physical resurrection.

We have given Mark's account of the resurrection careful treatment because it is, as far as we know, the original written source of the events of that first Easter Day involving the discovery of the empty tomb from which so many conclusions have been jumped to, especially that Jesus was physically returned to life again. Before turning to the texts of Matthew, Luke and John and their accounts of the story of the resurrection and the consequent appearances thereafter, we shall suggest a way of viewing them experientially.

Chapter 2
The Experience of Grief: An Aid to Interpretation

Having established that a different understanding of Mark 16.1–8 is necessary the issue of how to interpret and make sense of the stories contained in the remaining three Gospels becomes an important one.

We have all experienced the loss of loved ones because death is a universal and inescapable event. When someone close to us dies we feel deeply that part of ourselves has been lost too. The main subject/object of our love has been taken from us and a period of re-adjustment in our relationship occurs, however long or short that time has to be.

There are often sleepless nights in which the relationship with the deceased and perhaps the manner of death is turned over and over again in the mind. Lateness in retiring and early rising is common when the brain is numbed with grief in the initial stages of bereavement. For instance, at the resurrection the women are said to arrive early at the tomb, perhaps because they had been unable to sleep.

A cauldron of emotions is on the boil for a considerable duration: sense of loss, disbelief, confusion, shock, sadness, yearning, despair, humiliation, regret, anger, denial, thankfulness, questioning, fear, anxiety, guilt, recrimination, rumination and so on. The emotional mixture takes some time to sort out if ever. Traces of some of these emotions may be found in the Gospel stories.

In imagination and consciousness, the loved one is still there, perhaps sitting in a favourite chair, eating with us at table, accompanying us on a walk, sitting with us in a garden, or with us in other familiar places. Not there physically, but inescapably with us nonetheless, in a love which is indestructible. And when we socialise with other members of the family or a circle of friends, the 'missing' one often crops up in conversation, in reminiscences: "Do you remember when such and such happened...?" "He/She would have enjoyed that..." or "would have enjoyed doing such and such." There is sometimes a desire to remember at the place where a person died as seen, for instance, in the roadside shrines spontaneously created after a fatal accident and where flowers are still placed on the anniversary of the event. To go and sit in a garden and recall memories, to take a stroll along familiar pathways, to visit again a favourite haunt and other places where the loved one was known, are often indulgences which the bereaved may decide to re-experience, and on several occasions. Grief takes many forms, always individually expressed, and all valid, for each of us must grieve in the way that we feel the need so to do.

Psychologists, in the past, have attempted to systematise the grief process into various stages, whether three, four, five or even more depending upon a particular scholar's theory. For instance, Spiegal defines grief in five stages: shock, control, regression, adaptation, anticipatory.[5] But more recent studies have concluded that such categorisation is unrealistic and that grief is a much more complex experience than can ever be defined. Each person's grief experience is unique because reactions can vary depending on nature and nurture and social and cultural factors.

Two of the best contemporary examples of outpourings of grief stories are those following the death of Queen Elizabeth 2nd and before her, Prince Philip, Duke of Edinburgh, when members of the Royal Family and countless members of the public appeared on television to relate their reminiscences of them both, and to tell what happened when they met them, what they did, and how much they had achieved in their long lives, what their acquaintance of them meant and the immense influence they had upon them.

All of those who shared such stories were doing what human beings have always done when either a loved one or a significant person in their lives, dies. From such experiences, including our own, we may deduce that similar telling and retelling of stories occurred among the disciples and others, following the death of Jesus. Such, therefore, must be the nature of the appearance stories in the three Gospels which record them.

In the case of the disciples, their experience is quite complicated in a way that we shall never fully understand. Their loss was massive. It was the Messiah of long hope and expectation who had been crucified. Jesus died because of huge political and religious opposition, rejection by an entrenched establishment determined to obliterate him and his

---

[5]Spiegal Y. *The Grief Process. SCM. London. 1978. p59ff.*

teaching because of a perceived threat to their position. The disciples had found themselves so enthralled by this charismatic teacher that they had literally left all to follow him and now everything they had staked their lives upon was taken away. Not just them but perhaps several scores of 'camp followers' were also totally devastated. Their sense of loss cannot be overestimated and their feelings of devastation can never be fully comprehended.

Bearing our own experiences in mind, we may approach the Gospel stories of the 'appearances' of the 'risen' Jesus in a new way, viewing them as the grief experiences of the disciples, each having links with previous incidents in their relationship with Jesus as he practised his ministry and as they witnessed his deeds, heard his words and were involved with him in his various relationships and encounters with people of all kinds.

For instance, as we shall see later, the story of the catch of fish in John 21.1–14 echoes that of Luke 5.1–11 and Peter's confession story in John 21.15–19 has resonances with that in Matthew 16.13–20. The stories of the upper room appearances likewise must have a historic background because that was a familiar meeting place, if not the headquarters of the Jerusalem ministry. The story of Mary's tryst with Jesus in the garden, John 20.11–18, may also be based on previous meetings.

Re-viewing the resurrection in this way may evoke the accusation of speculation, but no more so than the way in which the stories are written at the moment and more often than not treated literally by scholars in their commentaries and preachers in their pulpits.

I have not yet found a commentary which does not, in

some way or other, treat the resurrection event as a literal, historical and physical fact, albeit capable of metaphysical interpretation, which it could not possibly be, especially from a realistic and scientific point of view. From the descriptions of Jesus' arrest, torture, crucifixion and burial, there is no way in which the physical body could be restored to life. He would be brain dead and decay would have begun to have set in.

The importance of both rationality and reality has been too readily underestimated in past treatments of the resurrection stories. A scientific approach involves the fact that, except for a few exceptional and sometimes unexplained circumstances, the laws of physics, chemistry, biology and physiology, etc. remain the same even though, over the centuries cultural and circumstantial perceptions of them, which used to be more primitive, have changed and developed. We are entirely justified in using our contemporary 'spectacles' to view events of long ago and to re-assess what really happened.

The resurrection stories imply that somehow (by divine intervention?) Jesus' body was acted upon by an external force and brought back to life. He was then able to appear here and there at will, travel several miles in the briefest of times, pass through solid structures, eat meals and hold conversations.

All of this defies credibility and contradicts what we know to be real and our own actual experience of life. Interpretations other than the traditional ones are called for, that is to regard the stories as those of grief experiences.

This approach also accords with the experiential interpretation of scripture because it helps us to get 'behind' the stories as they are written and to imagine, realistically, what actually happened in each situation and thereby bring credibility to the biblical accounts.

Chapter 3
Matthew's Embellishments

Matthew 28.1–10: The Mystery of the Missing Body: This is an account based on Mark 16.1–8 but embellished somewhat to persuade Matthew's Jewish readers of the veracity of a physical resurrection. At the tomb, the two Mary's (Magdalene and the mother of James, Mark 16.1) experience a convenient earthquake, a visiting 'angel' with the strength to roll away the loosened heavy tombstone and then to sit on it dressed in white. The guards are still there and are stiff with fright. The angelic mythological figure then invites the women to view the empty tomb and then to pass on the news that Jesus is to be found in Galilee where they will meet him again. Filled with awe and joy, the women run to tell the disciples. Jesus meets them in the way, greets them with a word of peace and allows them to fall at his feet, grab hold of him and worship him. He repeats the instruction to go to Galilee to where he is quickly transported in a mysterious manner.

There are differences from Mark; only two women and not four who go to look but not to anoint; the stone in Mark is already rolled away; there is a young man dressed in white (Mark himself?) not an angel, who passes on the message that

Jesus will meet them in Galilee. In Mark, the women are 'terrified' and say "nothing to anyone, because they were afraid." (Mar 16.8)

In Matthew, Jesus allows the women to touch him whereas in John's account Mary is forbidden to do so, again to reinforce the physicality of the resurrection and to stress its reality as a means of persuading faith. Matthew adds the note of joy, missing from Mark, but is guilty of "reading the Easter joy of the Church back into his account of the resurrection."[6]

It is assumed, in all the Gospel accounts, that the empty tomb itself is enough proof of the resurrection, whereas, logically, it is only proof that the body was gone.

The details added by Matthew strain credibility but were designed to reinforce the faith of the Jewish Christian communities post 70AD when, with the destruction of the Temple by the Romans an important focus of their religion was gone.

Matthew 28.11–15: The Guards' Report, True or False? The strong likelihood is that, according to law and custom, the body of Jesus, following crucifixion and burial, was taken from the tomb by Roman soldiers and flung onto the continuously burning rubbish heap outside Jerusalem known as Gehenna. This would be done to avoid potential for further unrest among the populace and to make sure that that was finally dealt with. Obviously, it would be convenient for the Jewish establishment if it could be believed that the disciples had taken the body away having bribed the Temple guards to say that it was done while they were asleep. The risk of execution for this misdemeanour would have to be

---

[6] Fenton J. C. *Saint Matthew. Pelican. 1963. p450.*

gainsaid. Post the fall of Jerusalem and the beginnings of a schism between Christians and Jews, it is understandable that Jewish Christians would want to play the blame game. The rumour, it seems, was widely current at the time amongst the scattered Jewish communities who felt under threat from the growth of the Christian presence.

Matthew 28.16–20: A Galilean Appearance: The great Commission: Was this hill in Galilee the site of the Sermon on the Mount, that of the Transfiguration, the Mount of Olives or another? No one knows! Somehow Jesus makes a rapid transit from Jerusalem to Galilee in the north of the country making this an unlikely historic scenario. Some scholars regard this as a later addition to tie up the Gospel and provide a more suitable ending rather than that of the guards' report. Memories of Jesus' teaching on mountains, remembered in time of grief, may have influenced this story.

In fact, mountains have a huge symbolic significance in the scriptures. To climb them is to encounter God, as with Moses and his reception of the divine commandments and the rest of the Law (Torah) (Ex. 20.1–17); as with Elijah retreating to be alone with God following his battle with idolaters (1Kings 19.1– 18); as with the Psalmist who looks to the hills as a sign of God's presence (Ps. 121.1).

With Jesus, his sermon preached on the mount gained a particular authority (Mt. 5–7); another mountain scene gave a confirmation of his ministry in the Transfiguration experience (Mt.16.1–13); and then the Mount of Olives was where he entered upon his passion (Lk. 22.39–45).

All of this is background to his 'appearance' on the mountain in Galilee where there was an assertion of his authority once again and the validation of his teaching, bearing in mind the resonances of those previous events.

The 'risen Jesus' is met with both worship and doubt which suggests that this 'appearance' is of the imagination for some of the eleven and not for others. Verses 18ff suggest a more developed theology than that which would exist in c33AD the time of the resurrection. The idea of the 'cosmic' Christ is implied; the missionary task is to all peoples (Jew and Gentile alike, post the controversy of Gentile admission); the Trinitarian formula is to be used for baptism, and the content of the teaching, contained presumably in this Gospel, is that to be by churches sympathetic to the Matthean tradition. The living presence of Christ is assured, always, as these missionary tasks are carried out, to the end of the age, that is, until the times of this world are brought to a conclusion. (A discussion of what this means, 'eschatologically' may be found elsewhere in chapter 8). Although not mentioned here, the Ascension, as found in Luke's Gospel, has to be assumed.

We note that Mark's Gospel, ending at 16.8 has no resurrection appearances. Matthew has two stories, probably selected from quite a number of others current at the time. Matthew seems to affirm the reality of the event, whereas 28.16–20, if written by another hand as some scholars believe, does not necessarily do so.

Chapter 4
Luke's Augmentations

Luke24.1–12: The Resurrection: In Luke's account the women are not numbered or named until later (vs. 10), the stone is discovered to have been already rolled away, and they go into the tomb and find no body. The one man of Mark and the angel of Matthew become two men dressed in 'shining apparel'. (In law two witnesses were required to verify such a discovery). The men assure the women that Jesus 'has been raised', i.e., his body has been acted upon in some way not excluding the possibility that the body has been lifted up and carried out of the tomb and disposed of. A retrospective prediction of Jesus is remembered (vs. 7) but this is an unrealistic statement for even Jesus himself, if he was genuinely human, would not be able to foretell the future. He may have guessed, with some degree of certainty, or may even have had a premonition, that he would be eventually put to death as a consequence of his life and ministry and especially as a result of his forthright comments about the ecclesiastical hierarchy.

The women's report back to the disciples is regarded as nonsense. A later edition of the text has Peter go examine the evidence for himself thus making sure that he gets a mention as 'leader' of the disciples. The passage, therefore, merely refers to the empty tomb, from which a resurrection may be inferred, but not conclusively so.

Luke 24.13–35: The Emmaus Road: This story is a prime example of what happens during 'grieving processes'. Bereaved people often imagine that the dear departed loved one is still with them. For instance, he/she is still sitting in his/her favourite chair and is talked with. In familiar situations and places the presence of the loved one is keenly felt. Absent in body they are present in mind and just as really so. Conversations with the loved one may still occur.

This writer once visited a woman recently bereaved who spoke fondly of her 'departed' husband yet affirming that he was still with her. She said, "When I go walking along the sea front each day I know that he is walking with me." It is in the light of such grief experiences that we must view the Emmaus Road narrative. There is no need to reproduce the story or to deal with it critically verse by verse. The conversation recorded here is what one would expect of bewildered people trying to make sense of the recent events in which they have been closely involved. Although Cleopas is not mentioned in the list of the 'twelve', he and his friend/wife(?) are described as 'followers', being among those, presumably, who were on the outer edge of the disciples' inner band. They debate with the unidentified stranger the events of recent days and ponder the reasons for them. Then it all clicks into place! It is to fulfil the prophecy. But in all honesty, we can no longer believe in prophecy in such a predictive way. The New Testament writers, with hindsight, selected verses from the Old Testament scriptures they knew which apparently foretold certain events in the life of Christ, sometimes with the flimsiest of connections. It may well be that some Old Testament writers expressed Messianic hopes but these are the natural result of deep yearnings for better times ahead expressing the need for a 'Saviour' of some kind. To believe otherwise is quite unrealistic.

Some of the disciples may have shared with Luke memories of actually walking with Jesus to Emmaus on occasion and engaging in conversation with him. It was the usual practise of mendicant teachers to walk with their students speaking with them as they went. So here assumptions about the resurrection are integrated with an earlier memory to create an imagined conversation which leads on to a way of understanding what had happened.

The desire of Cleopas and his companion to make sense of things in the time of their sorrow is a natural part of a normal grieving process. The story concludes with them inviting the stranger to a meal in their home. It is said that recognition dawned because of the familiar way in which he broke the bread and then he suddenly disappeared, just like that! The mind boggles. Unless one believes in the existence of ghostly apparitions then credibility is strained. Here are surely echoes of many previous meals which Jesus had shared with his friends, now recollected in time of grief.

Luke 24.36–49: Another Appearance: Cleopas and his companion return to Jerusalem to share this story, presumably at the disciples' familiar meeting place, the upper room in the city, when bingo, Jesus suddenly appears. He greets them with the common everyday salutation, "Peace be with you." They thought that he was a ghost and were terrified. Where this story came from the Lord only knows, as they say, but it contains many fantastic and unbelievable details. The invitation to examine physical evidence for the resurrection, by seeing and touching Jesus' scars, only goes to show that those present felt and experienced a real presence of some kind (vs. 39) and to recount this in a story was done to prove this, likewise the eating of the cooked fish. The only way they had of describing a spiritual reality was by means of presenting physical evidence.

Again, as in the previous story, Old Testament 'evidence' is adduced as specifically foretelling events which were fulfilled in the life experiences associated with the life of Jesus the Christ. We would again concur with the view that prophecy is forth telling and not foretelling, that is the proclamation in the present of what is believed to be the judgement and will of God upon and for any given situation. It is impossible for anyone to predict the future in exact detail, although possible to predict the future in general terms from current events. Elsewhere than in the prophets, the Old Testament was scoured for 'proof texts' by New Testament writers. Such methodology is quite suspect to the modern mind. The passage ends with the promise of the gift of 'power from above', to be received after a period of waiting in the city of Jerusalem. Luke foreshadows here the events of the Day of Pentecost, but that is another story!

Luke 24.50–53: A Necessary Parting: Writing this story about AD75+ and after emphasising the physicality of the resurrection, Luke now uses the device of an 'ascension' to ensure that Jesus has departed this world finally in order that as 'Holy Spirit' power he may return to the disciples/apostles in the near future. Bethany was the site of this departure; Acts ch.1 identifies the place as the 'Mount of Olives'. Jesus blesses the disciples, they worship him, then they return to the city filled with joy and give thanks in the Temple. which was still the locus of their fellowship and activity. In Judaistic mythology especially 'holy' people were assumed to have been taken into God or to have ascended in some way, e.g. Enoch and Elijah (Gen. 5.24; 2Kings 2.11), hence it was supposed that Jesus must have been also.

Thus Luke's accounts of the resurrection, which can be nothing other than an imagined physical presence, accords with our view that during their grieving process the minds of the disciples/apostles were filled with memories of their times with Jesus which, finding expression in these Gospel stories, give the impression of a concrete reality which is not actually the case. This leads us on to John's Gospel and to yet another complex scenario but not before a mention of Luke's further writings.

Postscript

The Acts of the Apostles, Being Luke's volume two, continues the story of the Jesus event and would perhaps be better named *The Acts of the Holy Spirit.*

Beginning where the Gospel concludes the *Acts* reprises, briefly, the resurrection story and tells of conversations with Jesus (1.3–11) before relating the experience of the Ascension.

According to 1.1, Theophilus would have read Luke's Gospel, then, following a short time, would have received the Acts. Most scholars agreeing the composition of both volumes c80–90AD, some 50–60 years after the discovery of the empty tomb, which makes it quite remarkable for Luke to

40

make the categorical statement in 1.3: "For forty days he (Jesus) appeared to them (the apostles) many times that proved beyond doubt that he was alive. They saw him and he talked with them about the kingdom of God."

Given the impossibility of a literal, historic resurrection we have to try to understand why such a bald statement was made. It can only be that a strong sense of the spiritual presence of Jesus was expressed in physical terms, as in other stories of resurrection appearances. To 'see' the risen Christ meant 'knowing' his real presence. This was so much so that the element of the resurrection of Christ was part of the *Kerygma,* the apostolic preaching, as C.H. Dodd observed in his renowned book *The Apostolic Preaching and its Developments,* (1935), although he does not deal with the issue of literal and physical resurrection and, like most scholars seem to do, accepts it as a given fact, albeit often with metaphysical and philosophical interpretations.

In actuality, we are making the case that it was not and that the explanation of 'grief stories' is much nearer the truth and that the unseen presence of the living Christ felt so real to the apostles and the other disciples that they expressed their experience of that presence physically and tangibly.

Chapter 5
John's Appendages

John 20.1–10: The Empty Tomb: It was against the law to visit a tomb on the Sabbath Day. It was possible to do so only after the first streaks of sunrise on the next morning. In this account, only Mary Magdalene discovers the empty tomb, the stone having already been rolled away, presumably by those who had removed the body, whoever 'they' were, possibly the Jewish temple Guard, Roman soldiers or even grave robber. She hastily reports the fact to Peter (at his domicile, perhaps the house of the Upper Room?) and 'the other disciple' (John?). John outruns Peter in the race to the tomb but hesitates to go in. He sees the linen wrappings lying inside. Peter, boldly as in character, does have the courage to enter and also witnesses the wrappings with the head cloth lying separately, tidily rolled up. It is not said that the wrappings themselves lie in tidy fashion. If two or three guards had removed the body of Jesus, we may surmise that they hastily removed and dumped them, but one of them, with a tidier disposition, had rolled up the head cloth neatly. We may discount, as unrealistic, the notion that the body of Jesus had somehow, phantom like, 'risen' through the grave clothes leaving them lying there in the tomb.

We are then told that the other disciple joined Peter in the tomb and that he saw and believed. It can only be that he verified for himself the fact that the tomb was empty. It is said that Peter and John still did not understand the predictive texts concerning the resurrection. (See chapter 6 for a discussion of these).

Verse 9 is problematic. We are not told which scriptures 'foretell' the rising of Jesus from the dead, but it is doubtful that they would predict the event any more than Isaiah 7.14 predicted the virgin birth. As the canon of New Testament scriptures had not yet been decided the scriptures must be from the Old Testament or the Apocrypha. Those usually suggested are Psalm 16.10, Hosea 4.2 and Jonah 1.17 and 2.1, but these are only viewed with the hindsight of a preconceived belief. Verse 10: the two disciples return home but Mary lingers at the tomb weeping her eyes out.

John 20.11–18: Mary and Jesus: Mary weeps because she believes that 'they' (the authorities?) have taken the body of Jesus away. This passage, we may understand, is a classic example of a grief story in which the bereaved person lingers at a scene with which the departed loved one has been associated and with whom a real but imagined conversation takes place based on a memory of a past meeting. We do not know the exact nature of the relationship between Jesus and Mary but previous Gospel incidents indicate that it must have been a close one. Mary of Magdala was one of whom much had been forgiven (Luke 7.42) and whose life was turned around by encounter with Jesus. There may or may not have been an actual gardener present then but communing with Jesus becomes predominant. Apparently, as he says, he is returning to his God (in the manner of an Elijah?) and the

43

disciples should be aware of this. Could this be John's version of the Ascension? In the story Mary is forbidden to touch Jesus, an intimation that she should not conceive of him in the way that she had known him in the past, i.e., by intimately touching him, as she had done in the anointing of his feet and wiping them with her hair (John 12.1–8) an incident, if recollected, again hints at this being a grief story.

John 20.19–23: The First Upper Room Experience: The grief stricken and perhaps guilt-ridden disciples, we assume, had locked themselves in the upper room, fearful, that they too, as associates of Jesus, may be arrested and put to death. The upper room as their regular Jerusalem 'headquarters' for some time, was a familiar meeting place. The salutation 'Peace be with you' was a greeting given, invariably, upon arrival to a home gathering. John 14 makes much of the peace which Jesus shared with the disciples, a peace which would remain with them after he had gone from them. Here they sense the peaceful presence of Jesus and felt joyful about the fact that his mission was not at an end. In John, this is a Pentecostal moment in which they experienced the gifting of the Holy Spirit enabling them to exercise a ministry of forgiveness. The story includes physical details of Jesus' injuries in order to emphasise the reality of his spiritual presence and to indicate that this was the same Jesus whom they had known previously. We may discount the idea that an apparition of Jesus passed through a solid and locked door as pure fantasy.

John 20.24–29: The Second Upper Room Experience: As the story has it, since Thomas was absent from the first meeting of the disciples on Easter Sunday evening, it was necessary for him to be persuaded of the reality of the spiritual presence of Jesus about which, in his grief, doubts had been expressed. He gathers with them a week later and Jesus appears, as if by magic, to invite him to touch him. What really happened must ever remain unknown, but in reality, it could not have happened as literally described. Was it a phenomenon of the grieving group mind? In the story Thomas is, however, persuaded by his sight of the wounds that somehow Jesus' presence is with them.

John 20.30–31: Why this book? In what most commentators believe was the original ending to John's Gospel, the author states his purpose for writing, 'so that the readers may believe'. The miracles/signs of the Gospel are intended to furnish proof that Jesus is the 'Messiah', the Son of the living God, but in fact they are nothing of the sort. Unusual events such as are described actually prove nothing at all apart from faith. Other people were reported to have performed similar deeds. Entrusting yourself to the way of Jesus and finding it to be true is the only way of knowing that he is 'Messiah'. Faith, as trust, involves discipleship, the practical day-to-day following in the way of Jesus.

SPECIAL NOTE: The Resurrection Story in John as the Ultimate Sign.

Much as Matthew's Gospel is structured around five blocks of Jesus' teachings so John's Gospel has, as its skeleton, the stories of the Seven Signs purportedly performed by Jesus, the first six leading dramatically to the seventh, that of the cross and resurrection taken together, seen as the 'glorification' of Jesus by the Gospel writer. The Seven Signs are:

1. Water Turned into Wine at the Cana Wedding, ch. 2.1–11 as a sign of the 'new wine' of the Gospel; his 'good news' for the people, as opposed to the traditional teaching of the religious establishment.

2. The Healing of the Official's son, ch. 4.46–54, as a sign of the new life available to both Gentile and Jew alike.

3. The Healing at the Pool of Bethesda, ch. 5.2–9, as a sign that the Sabbath is made for man and not man for the Sabbath (Mk. 2.27) i.e., the making of people whole is more important than the keeping of the Law, over which Jesus has supreme authority.

4. The Feeding of the Crowd, ch. 6.4–13, as a sign that Jesus is 'The Bread of Life' (vs.35), i.e., the successor to the Old Testament prophets who, in fulfilment of their expectations, had come to 'feed' the people with 'the word of God', Jesus himself being that word made flesh. The story of the provision of the manna in the wilderness, following the exodus, also has resonance here.

5. The Healing of the Blind Man, ch. 9.1–7, as a sign that Jesus is the 'giver of sight' to those who wish to 'see' in him the 'One sent from God'.

6. The Raising of Lazarus, ch. 11.1–44, as a sign that Jesus is the bringer of new life as opposed to the 'death' that people are living without true knowledge of God.

7. The Passion with the Resurrection, chs. 13–20 esp 19–20, as the climactic sign of Jesus, conqueror of death, which is the final destiny of all people, and also as the giver of the hope of a new life, forever.

The Gospel writer uses the stories 1–6 to make theological points. The stories are not capable of historical verification. Taken literally, they involve the use of extraordinary powers by Jesus, overriding the laws of nature in order to achieve a miraculous outcome for the benefit of recipients. The Logic involved seems to be: Jesus is the Son of God, the logos involved in the creation of the universe, therefore, he has power over the nature which is of his creation and so he may do anything he wishes.

The seventh sign is the climax of escalating displays of his power. In the cross, he takes on the powers of evil and death and in the resurrection, overcomes them. So Jesus is displayed as the original divine Superhero with extraordinary abilities. But this image contradicts the reality of the incarnation, in that he is conceived to be as fully human as the rest of us, subject to physical limitation in which if he did not die a full and final death then he could not have been the complete human being that he was/is believed to be. So the sign of the cross/resurrection in John cannot be other than symbolic to say that love conquers hate, life conquers death, truth conquers falsehood, goodness conquers evil, that eternity is more real than the world of time, the spiritual more than the physical. Since signs 1–6 are stories, the inference is that sign 7 is a story as well and could have been thought of as such originally, despite, perhaps, having some historical basis in the cross.

The "I am" Statements: These are also part of the structure of the Gospel and cannot be ignored. "I am" is of course redolent of the revelation of God's name and nature to Moses in the story of the encounter at the burning bush. The authority invested in Moses as liberator of the people is that of God Himself, His very nature and being, the eternal, active, mysterious Being.

"I am who I am…the One who is called 'I am' has sent me to you." (Ex. 3.14)

The "I am" sayings in John's Gospel, therefore, strongly imply that Jesus is the One sent from God as liberator of the people, as indeed he is reported as claiming to be (Luke. 4.18–19).

The sayings are: I am the Bread of Life (6.35), the Light of the World (9.5), the Door (10.9), the Good Shepherd (10.11), the Resurrection and the Life (11.25), the Way, the Truth and the Life (14.6), the True vine (15.1). Each one is a 'picture' illustrating, for popular consumption, an aspect of the nature of Jesus, leading into some truth about his work and witness on behalf of the Father who sent him into the world.

For our purposes, the most significant of the sayings is, "I am the Resurrection and the Life. Whoever believes in me will live, even though he dies. And whoever lives and believes in me will never die." (Jn. 11.25). This does not necessarily imply Jesus' own literal resurrection or a 'life after death' rather a new quality of life and living in the here and now.

John 21.1–14: The Lakeside, Appendix 1: The similarities in this story with those of Luke 15.1–11 lend credence to the view that this is a grief story. The disciples remember a significant event in their experiences of being with Jesus and transpose it to the time after his death. This is one of those times which is prominent in the memory and which could be said to have seemed as if it happened 'only yesterday'. Details may differ between the two stories but the overall similarity is of great significance.

Chapter 21 is regarded as a later supplement to the gospel

in any case so this story must have been included as further incidents from the life of Jesus are recalled by 'John' and are included in it.

In this story, the seven grief-stricken disciples have returned to Galilee (cf. Mark 16.7) and to the occupation they know best. As they fish, they recollect the time they had caught nothing after having fished all night.

Jesus had instructed them, from his vantage point on the shore, to fish differently and the nets became full. It was then, they remembered, how they had first become disciples. Now again on the shore of the lake, as they shared breakfast, it was as if Jesus was with them and they felt his presence near after casting their nets differently in order to enjoy success. Various suggestions have been made as to why the number of fish caught was said to be 153. The number is quite specific, avoiding approximations. Although several allegorical interpretations have been posed, it is likely that it represents the known number of fish at that time as recorded by Greek zoologists, thus symbolising the breadth of humanity and the inclusiveness of the Church in its gathering in of the peoples as a result of its mission. In Matthew 13.47 the net thrown into the sea gathers fish of every kind, thus a possible memory of the teaching of Jesus is here recollected and recorded as part of a grief story.

Here again the physicality of Jesus' presence and activity is imagined in order to emphasise the reality of his spiritual presence. Details are included in order to lend credibility to the story. This could be a sacramental allusion in that a physical and material description is intended to convey a spiritual reality.

John 21.15–19: Peter is Restored – Appendix 2: This story, with its threefold interrogation of Peter and his responses by way of his re-affirmations of love, is probably to reassure him (and readers of the Gospel) of his position as 'leader' of the disciples/apostles and to commission him, as figurehead of the others, to be a shepherd of Christ's sheep. If the Gospel was written c95AD+, and according to tradition, Peter died c65AD, then verses 18f are descriptive, having been written retrospectively from memory.

There are echoes here of the story in Matthew 16.13–20 in which Peter recognises Jesus for who he is and, in words that have been the subject of great debate, Jesus then commends him for his faith insight, which is the rock foundation on which the Church is to be built, thus apparently implying that Peter has some kind of primacy over the other disciples. So there are underlying links here with John's grief story.

Once again, the physicality of Jesus' presence and activity is imagined in order to emphasise the reality of his spiritual presence with details which are included to lend credibility to the story.

John 21.20–24: What about him? Is there a hint of Jealousy in Peter's question? The beloved disciple, probably John, was physically close to Jesus at the Last Supper in the upper room (John 13.21–29) and had asked the identity of the betrayer. Did Peter feel that his primacy was threatened?

Jesus' reply inferred that what had transpired between John and himself was no concern of Peter's. Peter should pay attention to his own discipleship, "Follow Me."

Under the influence of grief there is a confluence between the sense of the presence of Jesus at the lakeside and the memory of the final meal in the upper room.

John 21.24–25: There's a lot more to be said: John, if it is he, asserts his identity as the author of the Gospel plus this extra chapter. Countless scrolls would be inadequate to record the events of the life of Jesus. The Gospel ends, finally for a second time.

It is unusual for commentators not to treat the resurrection as a literal, historical and physical event despite sophisticated allusions and interpretations. The reality must be plainly re-stated that Jesus died, was buried and his body taken away by human agency and disposed of. The Gospel accounts of his 'appearances', when treated experientially, are grief stories recollected and recorded to lend meaning to the death of Jesus and subsequent events. This is the only way to make real sense of the passages in the four Gospels, one which coheres with a modern scientific way of looking at the world.

Chapter 6
The Predictive Texts

Those who take a more literal approach to the scriptures usually adduce texts in which, apparently, Jesus looks to his own resurrection as an event which is bound to happen historically.

On three specific occasions in the Synoptic Gospels Jesus 'foretells' his death and resurrection.

1. **Following the Petrine Confession.** Jesus, as Messiah, (Son of Man) in delineating His role declares that He must suffer and die before rising again on the third day, a suggestion which is resisted by the disciples. (Mark 8.31–38; Matthew 16.21–28; Luke 9.22–27)

2. **Following the Healing of the Epileptic Boy.** Jesus chides the disciples for their failure, in their unbelief, to heal an epileptic boy, inferring that they also do not believe Him when He speaks of His death and resurrection. (Mark 9.31–32; Matthew 17. 22–23; Luke 9.43b–45)

3. **Following the Encounter with the Rich Young Ruler/Prince.** One theory is that this is Prince

Agrippa, nephew of King Herod Antipas. Jesus commends the law-abiding wealthy young aristocrat for his quality of life but cannot persuade him to forsake his riches and follow Him, before speaking a third time about His impending death and resurrection. In Matthew's Gospel, the story of the generous owner of the vineyard intervenes. (Mark 10.32–34; Matthew 20.17–19; Luke 18.31–34)

Other 'mentions' of Jesus' death and/or resurrection are:

4. **The Triumphant Appearance of the Son of Man.** This is an apocalyptic post resurrection figure who will come to earth to rule in triumph and judgement. (Mark 13.24–27; Matthew 24.29–31; Luke 21.25–28)

5. **The Sign of Jonah.** Jesus apparently predicts here that as Son of man He will 'spend three days and nights in the depths of the earth' just as Jonah spent the same time inside the big fish, being an inexact allusion of the Gospel writers to the period between the death of Jesus on Good Friday and the discovery of the empty tomb on the third day. (Matthew 12.39–40; Luke 11.29–30) The story is missing from Mark, the earlier tradition.

6. **The Anointing by Mary.** Jesus, entering upon his passion experience, anticipates the imminence of His own death. He declares that the anointing of His feet by Mary is a preparation for His burial. (Mark 14.3–9; Matthew 26.6–13; John 12.1–8)

7. **John's Gospel.** In John's Gospel, written c95AD, a theologically more developed Gospel than the

Synoptics, allusions to the death and resurrection of Jesus are more nuanced and subtle. The Son of Man must be lifted up like the snake on the pole in the wilderness (3.14, see also 12.32–33. cf. Numbers 21.8–9). The authorities begin to plot the death of Jesus (5.18). The risen Son of Man will be the judge of all (5.27). The story of the feeding of the five thousand is treated in a Eucharistic manner, Christ being the Bread of Life, His flesh being given that the world may live (6.35ff). There is the promise that as Son of Man He will raise others on the last day, presumably because He has been raised Himself (6.44). Jesus is feeling the growing threat of His death (7.1, 19). He begins to speak about His 'going away' (8.21). He is the Good Shepherd willing to die for His sheep (10.1–17). The word of Thomas, "Let us go with Him that we may die with Him" is not a reference to the crucifixion but to the threat of stoning by some people for His 'blasphemy' (11.16–18, cf. 10.31–33).

The saying, "I am the resurrection and the life," (11.25) one of the seven 'I am' sayings which form the skeleton of the Gospel, and related to the, "I am that I am" of Exodus, is to be interpreted non-literally, rather metaphorically and spiritually. It is linked to Martha's own confession of faith (11.27). Caiaphas prophesies and plans Jesus' death which he would help to bring about. (11.49–53). The Palm Sunday story is one that is remembered when Jesus was 'raised to glory' (12.16).

In conversation with Greeks, Jesus views His death as a

grain of wheat falling into the ground (12.20–26). In chapters 14–16, Jesus speaks of both His going away and His return, "In a little while you will not see me, then a little while later you will see me." (16.16) In Chapter 17, the Great Prayer, Jesus prays for the disciples' future welfare and their work in the world, on the assumption that beyond His forthcoming death they will ultimately see His glory. (For further discussion of resurrection and eschatology, see chapter 8).

Conclusions: It is a fact of human experience that the future cannot be predicted although it may be conjectured. The cynical comment of Henry Ford that 'history teaches us that history teaches us nothing' is far from true.

Lessons may be learned from the past. Similar situations may help in guessing what may happen in the future, but certainty is always elusive and the unexpected may happen. In the Old Testament some of the prophets were right about the future and others were not but only the passage of time can help tell the difference between the true and the false.

Jesus could guess, with some degree of certainty, as a result of growing opposition from the authorities that they would connive at His death. But apart from the impossibility of a literal, physical, historic resurrection, He could not predict such an event without a supernatural knowledge of the future. If He could, and if He was not subject to human limitations in this regard, the incarnation itself was a sham.

In the Gospels, therefore, such predictions of Christ's resurrection comprise of a combination of retrospective material and an imposition of hindsight designed to verify existing assumptions. The apocalyptic passages are evidence of a Church still strongly influenced by Judaism and of a level of belief in the primitive Christian communities from which the written Gospels emerged. The question remains as to how the sight of an empty tomb morphed into the assumption of a resurrected body?

Chapter 7
Paul's Recapitulations

Acts 9.1–8: The Damascus Road Clue

Crucial to our understanding of the nature of the resurrection of Jesus Christ is the record of the appearance to Saul (later Paul) on the road to Damascus. Saul was vehemently against the Jesus sect. He was, by upbringing and belief, a strict Pharisee of the Pharisees (Phil. 3.5–6).

He is initially mentioned as a supporter of the stoning of Stephen, the first Christian martyr (Acts 7.58). Horrified by the rapid spread of the Jesus movement from its base in Jerusalem, he sought authority from the temple establishment to go and deal with the Christians in Damascus. His intense vehemence in this venture of persecution cannot be overestimated.

Whilst travelling on that road to Damascus with fellow supporters, there was an extraordinary event. A radical moment of enlightenment occurred as symbolised in the story by an intensely dazzling light. It was an encounter with the Risen Christ himself with whom Saul had a conversation, partly overheard by his accompanying cohort (Acts 9.1–10). Jesus, the person in the vision, questioned Saul as to the reason for persecuting him and then instructed him to continue his journey into the city and await further instructions.

The content of the encounter must have been shared first hand by Paul with St Luke as he gathered material to compile the Book of the Acts. We can do nothing but take his word for it and accept the description of what happened, it being an ultimately inexplicable experience, in which Paul became completely transformed in his attitude towards Jesus and the Christian movement. In the city he received counselling from Ananias, (Acts 9.10–19) a man also said to have received visionary instructions according to Luke's account.

The significant thing for us to note is that this was an appearance of the Risen Christ, but **without a physical body.** The effect upon Saul was of the nature of a spiritual, psychological, emotional, and intellectual life transforming experience.

This particular appearance helps us in our perceptions relating to the Gospel accounts which we have come to believe are possibly grief stories of events leading us through to the Day of Pentecost which we may now understand as a 'Damascus Road' moment in the experience of the disciples. By the time the Pentecost Festival had arrived they were at a peak in the their complex vortex of emotions and were ready for their moment of corporate enlightenment in the upper room, an event which proved to be an intense visionary experience for them and thus the source of their deep motivation for their forthcoming missionary endeavours. This was their one and only such encounter with the Risen Christ, one which was 'body' less. We shall return to the experience in a later chapter (11) and examine it in greater detail.

The Corinthian Contribution: 1 Corinthians 15.3–8:
This letter, written c54AD is the first known written reference to the resurrection of Jesus Christ. It was a tradition which Paul said that he had received (vs. 3,4), as was the 'information' that Jesus appeared to Peter and then to all the twelve apostles, (vs. 5) actually eleven assuming not to Judas, unless there is a story here of which we have no knowledge, or unless Matthias is included (Acts 1.26). Then there is a mention of an appearance to 500 disciples most of whom, 20 years or so after the event, are still alive, presumably willing to testify to it (vs. 6), with yet further appearances to James and again to all the apostles (vs. 7).

Then Paul claims an appearance to himself referring to the experience of the Damascus Road (Acts 9.1–19 and the days following.)

This leaves us seeking an explanation for the appearances mentioned in verses 4–7. We have no idea where this 'tradition' came from which was passed on to Paul. Presumably, he had picked up the stories orally circulating at the time in Jerusalem and other places. Our re-viewing of the accounts recorded in the four Gospels and the conclusions we have reached still apply irrespective of whether or not people in the Christian communities came to believe in a literal, physical, historic resurrection event. The conclusions drawn from the fact that the tomb was empty had led to the growth of the resurrection myth and subsequent appearance stories, based on remembered incidents from the disciples' shared life with Jesus.

Paul mentions the appearance to the 500 and to James neither of which are to be found in the Gospels. The appearance to the 500, especially, at some mass event or other is obviously quite difficult to believe. Here again, Paul's source is unknown.

1 Corinthians 15.12–58 then leads into a discussion about matters for which there is no concrete evidence. The resurrection of Christ is said to be certain proof of our own resurrection, an assertion which defies the rules of logic in that it generalises from the particular. If we see one single brown cow in a field we cannot, therefore, infer that all other cows are brown, which manifestly they are not. Hence the 'fact' that one person has 'risen' does not mean that others will be. Paul then discusses the nature of our existence beyond death, obviously before the present physiological knowledge that we have now. We cannot envisage any form of existence beyond death which is not related to the chemical activity of the brain. Once we are brain dead then we are not alive in any sense of which we are aware. We do not yet know of any form of consciousness independent of brain function. If we discover that there is, then it will be a pleasant surprise and any anticipation, in faith, of that possibility, will have been justified.

Chapter 8
Resurrection and Return

The subject of eschatology is not a simple one and is the cause of much controversy and division. Different views abound. In the New Testament mythology of resurrection, it was thought that Jesus died to rise again and then ultimately to return again at the consummation of history as influenced by Jewish apocalyptic beliefs.

At the heart of the matter is how we regard and use scripture. In this I would draw a distinction between the 'literal' and 'literary' approaches. The first takes scripture in a straightforward way accepting the words as they are printed and believing that they are 'The Word of God'. The second approach investigates the background and the context of any given book or passage, recognising the nature of its literary form and also that truth is mediated to us in a variety of different ways bearing in mind the culture which has influenced the writer. Today we must also take into account developments in other disciplines such as science, sociology, anthropology, history and so on which can also shed light upon our scriptures.

Moreover, there is a need to be consistent in our approach. For instance, we readily accept that the Genesis stories of creation are mythological in the positive sense of that word, i.e., as vehicles of important truth but not necessarily in a factual scientific sense. This means that eschatological passages must be treated similarly and that we must seek for the truth within the 'myth' of a messiah descending from the heavens in spectacular fashion. Again, I emphasise that I use the term positively. In ancient times myth was used as a way of understanding the world and the cosmos, as human beings wrestled to come to terms with the meaning of their existence. In our own time the cultural milieu is more scientific and analytical.

This brings us to the scientific view of the 'end times' for the human race. Latest calculations predict that the sun will grow so hot that life on earth will become impossible between 1.75 and 3.25 billion years from now. The planet Mars will then fall into the habitable zone of our solar system so that the human race will need to establish a presence there. But this only delays the end for us as the sun will die by burning itself out in around 6 billion years by which time, we humans will need to have found another habitable planet elsewhere in our galaxy or beyond. The death of the sun, and consequently of our solar system will happen as a matter of course because that is the way the universe has been created and programmed.

Whether the end will come before then as a result of a cataclysmic divine intervention is up to anyone to believe but is highly unlikely. God does not have such a history of intervention. He neither causes nor prevents earthquakes, tsunamis, volcanic eruptions and other phenomena. These are not deliberately inflicted upon the world by Him as some kind of judgement but happen as a result of geological factors. The end will come as a result of the natural order of things, fortunately for us, at some vastly remote time in the future unless climate change brings it about as a result of the human ill treatment of planet earth.

So, we are led to consider the origins of the notion of the coming of a Messiah, which roots are to be found in the Old Testament. Because of the tough times God's people experienced as the underdog of the Middle East, a conviction grew among them that one day God Himself would step in and award them their 'rightful' place among the nations. The agent of such a glorious assertion of divine intervention would be a Messianic figure of towering and irresistible strength. Apocalyptic passages such as those in Daniel 7–12 speak of a Day of the Lord when the judgement of the nations will occur although Amos warns that such judgement will begin with Israel. The presiding judge on behalf of God will be the 'Son of Man', a figure possessed of dazzling and terrifying glory.

It was natural that because the early Church had its roots in Judaism, it would continue to believe that there would be a consummation of history in this way. Such Messianic expectations were attached to Jesus Christ whose imminent return was expected. The fact that, at times, Rome and its Caesars gave the Church a hard time, encouraged such an apocalyptic belief.

However, in what could be said to be the more authentic gospel passages, because they are not apocalyptic, Jesus eschews such notions of power and grandeur, principally in the Temptations (Matt. 4.1–11; Lk.4.1–13). He is also said to refuse those who would take him and make him King (Jn.6.15), and to resist recruiting legions of angels to save him from the cross (Matt.26.51–53). Also, Peter is told that swords are not to be used (Lk. 22.49–51). Displays of power and triumphalism are not the way of Jesus. Indeed, the passage of scripture which seemed to mean much to the early Church was that of Isaiah 53, a far from triumphal description of the role of the messiah, rather that of an inglorious suffering servant, significantly, contrary to eschatological expectations.

Furthermore, I believe we may regard passages such as the Little Apocalypse (Mk. 13) as not necessarily part of the original teaching of Jesus, but evidence of an early Church still influenced by Judaism. They have nothing in common with those parables of the kingdom which concentrate on societal transformation.

St Paul, likewise, retained strains of the apocalyptic, (e.g. in 1 Thess. 5.1–11) initially believing in an imminent return of a triumphant Christ to exercise a punitive kind of judgement. He later revised his views on such a coming, postponing it to an indeterminate date in the future.

So where does this lead us as we search for a relevant theology of eschatology for today? The original meaning of the mythology needs to be influenced by our contemporary knowledge of the cosmos. We may believe in a Living Christ (God) who comes to us at every moment in time until whatever distant end occurs. His coming is to be discovered, not in some spectacular and cataclysmic event at an unknown future date, but in the here and now, as God's people, together with those who are for us and not against us, realise his kingdom on earth as it is in heaven – a kingdom of justice, freedom and peace based on the two great commandments of love.

This is not necessarily the last word on eschatology! Other views will emerge as scholarship advances, but hopefully this will do as a provisional statement.

Chapter 9
Is God Interventionist?

The crucial question with regard to both the doctrines of the virgin birth and the resurrection is, "Is God interventionist?" as indeed to other important Christian doctrines and opinions, not least that of intercessory prayer.

With respect to the resurrection itself, we need to ask, "Did God in some way or other act upon the definitely dead body of Jesus sealed in the tomb, bring it back to life and then roll the stone away to let him escape so as to make several appearances to the disciples by travelling great distances in an instant, pass through locked doors, eat bread and fish, etc. before 'ascending' up to heaven?"

These days, surely, these things belong to the world of fantasy, *Harry Potter* and the *Game of Thrones*, the realm of imagination and not of reality.

The factual evidence is overwhelmingly in support of the view that God is not overtly interventionist. For instance, humanity has appeared on the 'cosmic clock' at one minute to midnight and has proceeded to pollute and exploit planet earth which has been about 13.7 billion years in the making (that since the big bang), and 3.7 billion of those specifically to do with the earth itself.

God has not intervened to stop the human destruction of his creation.

Again, refugees abound in their millions, homeless, starving, oppressed, in their camps in Jordan, Bangladesh and elsewhere, not to mention the thousands crossing the English Channel in search of a better life. Heinous injustices are perpetrated for political, racial and religious reasons in many parts of the globe by one group of people upon another or by the powerful over the powerless. The latest and most horrific example is the invasion of Ukraine at the instigation of Vladimir Putin and his dream of re-establishing the Greater Russia. Despite the fervent prayers of some Christians, there has been no divine intervention to rebuff this military action with all its attendant atrocities. God has not intervened to correct any of these situations. He leaves it to us humans to address them appropriately.

We may therefore conclude that God is not obviously interventionist and there is no evidence to suggest that He is. It may be believed that he is but this is quite mistaken. Certain favourable events and circumstances may seem to suggest that this is the case, but if so then unfavourable situations would have to be attributed to Him also. This is actually something which parts of the Old Testament do, viewing God as responsible for both the good and the bad in the history of His 'chosen people', a concept which itself infers a great deal of interventionism, entirely unproven and unjustified.

In British history also, there has been an element of 'God is on our side' particularly relating to the threat of German military expansionism that was the cause of two world wars. Churchill's favourite hymn apparently was 'Onward Christian soldiers', sung with reference to our army. The

Dunkirk evacuation was an 'Act of God' especially as Hitler did not follow up immediately with an invasion. The Battle of Britain, when the few fought against the massive superiority of the Luftwaffe and won, has also by some, been attributed to divine influence.

But here again there is no evidence to support such convictions or to bolster any view which favours one nation or race or group of people over another. As Jesus said, the sun and the rain shine and fall upon just and unjust alike. God has no favourites; all are equally loved.

Moreover, if it were the case that some were more favourably regarded than others and God acts on their behalf, then not only would it mean that He was unjust, but that He would contradict Himself by denying the very gift of the free will invested in humanity. One characteristic that we do expect of God is that He would be consistent.

On an individual level, the way that God seems to 'answer' prayer is often a real issue. A desirable outcome may be prayed for but it does not happen. People with cancer are often prayed for, some live and some die and it is often wondered why. God does not intervene in either case. It all depends on the medical conditions pertaining to each individual and the treatments available and their effectiveness.

Praying for divine intervention, which is unavailable, is mistaken, rather to pray that whatever the outcome of an illness, God's loving presence may be experienced in the knowledge that he is sharer in our suffering, sorrowing and grieving. Having said that, it does seem rather unfair that a Christian who has been prayed for should die and an atheist who has not been prayed for should live, examples which appeared on television some years ago. It is important to recognise the complexity of the issue and the fact that there are no easy answers, but this only serves to intensify the perplexity involved in attempting to understand the ways of God's providence. It is often believed that "God moves in mysterious ways His wonders to perform." Yes, inexplicable events do happen but, one day, due to the advances made in human knowledge, explanations may be found. New understandings of natural laws, hitherto unknown, are being discovered as time goes by, the inexplicable becoming explicable.

In 2006, there was published the result of an experiment in prayer by a consultant cardiologist Dr Herbert Benson, director of the Mind/Body Medical Institute, Boston USA. He arranged for certain of his patients to be prayed for with regard to their healing. Where strangers prayed unknowingly for their patients there was no beneficial effect. There was a slight improvement in those patients who knew that they were being prayed for, but the difference was not appreciable so, therefore, the results were inconclusive and attributed to psychological reasons. There was no evidence of divine intervention in either case. But either way, whether healing takes place as the apparent result of prayer or whether it does not, there is no evidence to support the view that God is, in any way, interventionist.

This is because the laws of nature, of cause and effect, operate with consistency under normal conditions, otherwise our very existence would, in the first place, be impossible and in the second place greatly insecure. It is difficult not to believe therefore, that in the case of the death of Jesus Christ, by one of the most hideous punishments ever devised, it was not absolutely final, especially as the Gospels report, a spear was thrust into his side to ensure that his life was completely ended. The natural physical laws of death would takeover, the brain would cease to function and every vestige of consciousness gone.

If God is not interventionist then that indeed was Christ's end and the incarnation a reality, in that he died the death of us all with an incontrovertible finality.

So the phenomenon of the resurrection has to be understood in ways other than that of a literal, physical, historic event. It has to have been rather a profound life changing spiritual experience which led the apostles, and others, to a realisation that the Spirit of Christ is alive and at work in the world both then and for always. In the present world, as at the time, the only divine intervention is that which occurs when human beings, in co-operation with the ever-present Spirit of Christ, act on God's behalf. He has no hands but our hands to do His work today.

To an understanding of what actually happened at the resurrection, we shall return in chapter 11. Meantime it will be worth our while to consider the views of several significant theologians.

Chapter 10
What Some Theologians Say

It will be useful to summarise the views of some major theologians with regard to the resurrection as part of our search for a valid view. Here are a few:

Karl Barth (1886–1968)

His theology was basically 'Christocentric', in other words he believed that every aspect of theology should relate to Jesus Christ as Word of God incarnate. His twelve volume *Church Dogmatics* was an unfinished life-long achievement encompassing his theological journey. In symphonic fashion, he returns to the same themes several times, not least his views on the Person and Work of Jesus Christ. His later views on the resurrection are naturally of our concern here. A website on Barth by Wyatt Houtz quotes from *Church Dogmatics 3.2:*

"The empty tomb is not the same thing as the Resurrection…it is only its presupposition. Hence it is only a sign, although an indispensable sign. Christians do not believe in the empty tomb but in the Living Christ. This does not mean however that we can believe in the Living Christ without believing in the empty tomb. Is it just a legend? Rejection of the empty tomb has always been accompanied by the rejection of the saga of the living Jesus. Far better, then, to admit that the empty tomb belongs to the Easter event as a sign."

Barth therefore, neither denies the historicity of the empty tomb nor attempts to describe a physical resurrection, rather to assert it as a vital spiritual experience of the Living Christ, which, being of a mystical nature is beyond definition.

"How the tomb became empty is immaterial, it remains a sign of a greater reality, and whatever the nature of the resurrection it is, by God's grace, a justification of Christ and his person and work and thereby a justification of humankind." (C.D. 4.1)

Rudolf Bultmann (1884–1976)

He is best known for his work on demythologisation and the need for an existential interpretation of the New Testament which sat loose to historical issues. He is known to have said that, "the only two things we know for sure about Jesus Christ are that he was born and that he died, all else being myth." He does not view the resurrection therefore as an historical event which helps us to understand the meaning of the cross, nor as a miracle which has to be verified to give credence to the significance attached to it by the Church. The records of the resurrection appearances are 'incredible', the real miracle being the rise of faith in the disciples. He describes the resurrection as, "the self-manifestation of the Risen One, the act of God in which the saving event of the cross is completed."[7]

The resurrection is real for Bultmann in that we encounter the living Christ by faith. But in describing the resurrection as an 'act of God' he is subscribing to an interventionist view of God which we would question (see chapter 9). He does not, therefore, completely jettison the idea of the resurrection as being an historic event, but that we may believe in the presence of the living Christ without accepting any need for a physical, historic resurrection. Existentially, said Bultmann, it is through our decision for Christ that we pass ourselves over from an inauthentic to an authentic existence, with little or no need to accept the mythological trappings of the gospels. He does not say how and in what sense the presence of the Living Christ is with us.

Dietrich Bonhoeffer (1906–1945)

Bonhoeffer is one of the twentieth century's heroes of faith, known for his active resistance to Hitler and Nazism which resulted in his eventual martyrdom. Influenced by Barth his theology was fairly conventional although expressed in original ways. During his imprisonment, however, as seen from his *Letters and Papers from Prison* radical ideas such as the notion of 'religionless Christianity' and 'man come of age' began to emerge which his death prevented from coming to fruition.

Insofar as the resurrection is concerned, he appears not to be too concerned about historicity, the story of it being real

---

[7] Bultmann R. *Jesus and the Word. Collins. Fontana. London. 1958.* p40.

enough.

"This mythology (resurrection and so on) is the thing itself."[8]

"Only the Risen One makes possible the presence of the living Person and gives the necessary presupposition for Christology."[9]

"When we have Christ witnessing to himself in the present, any historical confirmation is irrelevant."[10]

"What is the meaning of the news of the empty tomb before the news of the resurrection? Is it the deciding fact of Christology? Was it really empty? If it was not empty then Christ is not risen and our faith futile? It looks as though our faith in the resurrection were bound up with the news of the empty tomb. Is our faith then ultimately only faith in the empty tomb? Empty or not empty, it remains as a stumbling block. We cannot be sure of its historicity."[11]

"To live in the light of the resurrection, that is the meaning of Easter."[12]

But what if, as he has said, 'the mythology is the thing itself', is it merely a myth on the pages of the Gospels, or something more real than that?

---

[8] Bonhoeffer. *Christology.* Collins. Fount. London. 1975 p14.
[9] Ibid. p44.
[10] Ibid. p73.
[11] Ibid. p112
[12] Ibid. p85.

Hans Kung (1928–2021)

In his book *On Being a Christian* Kung treats the resurrection as symbolic. Christ's death was real enough, the question is how did the new beginning of the Church come about? How did Jesus become the content of its proclamation that is, proclaimed as alive and one known to be active in the present? The Christian Faith stands or falls by the resurrection which contradicts all scientific thinking as well as all ordinary convictions and experiences[13], the difficulty being, "there is no one in the whole of the New Testament who claims to have been a witness of the resurrection. It is nowhere described."[14] The New Testament Easter documents, "are not meant to be testimonies to the resurrection, but testimonies to the raised and risen Jesus. Nor can the stories in the Gospels be harmonised."[15] So how does Kung view the event? He goes on to say:

"Resurrection is the fact that God intervenes at the point where everything is at an end, [to bring about] the beginning of new life out of death…It is a radical transformation into a wholly different state [and] into another unparalleled definitive immortal life…The reality of the resurrection itself therefore is completely intangible and unimaginable. Resurrection and Raising are pictorial expressions; they are images, metaphors, symbols which correspond to the thought-forms of that time."[16]

---

[13] Kung H. *On Being a Christian.* Collins. Fount. Glasgow. 1978. p346

[14] Ibid. p346

[15] Ibid. p350.

[16] Ibid. p350

Kung does not, therefore, regard it as an historical event, verifiable by research, but "It has certainty for faith as a real event."[17]

Is it therefore one of the ten impossible things we have to believe before breakfast? Is it a non-event, except in imagination? Is it believable only because it is a good thing to believe? Is it a myth like all the others in the Bible, which may or may not have historical foundation? Nevertheless, an event attributable to divine intervention! One is led to the conclusion that there is something of a contradiction here.

Michael Goulder (1927–2010)

It will be good to include the thoughts of this Jewish theologian who has greatly helped in our understanding of the Hebraic background to the life and ministry of Jesus, specifically in the book *This Hebrew Lord* by Bishop Jack Spong who rates him highly. Goulder is quite frank in his views: "The appearances [of the risen Jesus] are to be explained psychologically. The concrete physical details arise from disputes within the Church."[18] He cites examples of melodramatic 'conversion' experiences and stories of ecstatic visions and 'encounters with Christ'. In the scriptures, there are accounts of Isaiah's vision of God, Peter's vision in the Book of Acts and that of St Paul on the Damascus Road.

"It is characteristic of such experiences that they occur at the deep crises of life and seem intensely real."[19] They are the

---

[17] Ibid. p350
[18] In chapter 3 of ed. D'Courte G. *Resurrection Reconsidered, 'The baseless Value of a Vision'.* One World, Oxford. 1996.p48
[19] Ibid. p50

result of a complex psychological process, not yet fully understood, the roles of guilt and pressures of circumstances being of significance. He also cites examples of collective visionary experiences (delusions?) such as those at Knock in Ireland and Lourdes in France.

He goes on, "We do not need both a natural and a supernatural explanation for any phenomena. Experience shows that we should always prefer the natural hypothesis or we shall fall into superstition."[20]

Goulder therefore believes, not without some scientific justification, that the resurrection was a corporate psychological visionary experience of some kind, albeit described in physical terms to lend the appearance stories a particular credibility.

Dan Cohn-Sherbok (1945)

He is Professor Emeritus of Judaism at the University of Wales.

In the aforementioned symposium *The Resurrection of Jesus* another Jewish theologian Dan Cohn-Sherbok expresses the view that there is no evidence for the resurrection of Jesus Christ as the findings of contemporary science afford no objective evidence for it. It is purely a subjective psychological experience. He waits for the evidence to emerge and would want it to be in the public domain witnessed by a large number of people.[21]

One has to agree that for such an important event God

---

[20] Ibid. p55
[21] See Chapter 12 in ed. Cousta G.D. *The Resurrection of Jesus.* Oxford. 1996. p184ff.

should have provided more conclusive evidence before a 'great cloud of witnesses', so verdict on God – could do better!

A.J.M. Wedderburn (1942)

He is the Retired Professor of New testament at the University of Munich.

In his book *Beyond Resurrection*[22] he expresses the view that the appearance stories, whatever they describe, "were not experiences of the resurrection, the raising of Jesus itself, rather inferences from the evidence set before them, e.g. they saw the empty tomb and inferred from it that Jesus was 'risen', or they had certain different kinds of experiences and inferred from them that Jesus was 'risen'."[23]

With regard to the New Testament documentation, chronologically speaking, it was Paul who first claims to have 'seen' the risen Jesus but this occurred later than the time of the Gospel stories, which were written down some forty or fifty years afterwards.

"It is a mistake to treat the stories as objective history when they are really subjective experiences, mystical and ecstatic in nature."[24]

N.T. Wright (1948)

He was formerly Bishop of Durham but since 2010 Professor of New Testament and Early Christianity at the

---

[22] SCM Press. London. 1999
[23] Wedderburn A.J.M. *Beyond Resurrection.* SCM Press.
London.1999. p67.
[24] Ibid. p67.

University of Aberdeen.

Tom Wright maintains belief in the stories of the appearances of the resurrected Christ literally as real events.

"I don't understand why you can't get to resurrection if you have an empty tomb and somebody is clearly there palpably alive again, inviting you to touch him and eating broiled fish."[25]

This is an incredible statement by a very gifted and intelligent scholar which denies all our scientific knowledge about the processes of death. The serious injuries inflicted upon Jesus meant that he was well and truly dead and beyond any recovery at all. Wright may be versed, as he is, in the biblical texts and historical scholarship, but he cannot ignore the findings of other academic and practical disciplines. Would he take the Genesis myths and stories like the ascension of Elijah so literally? He underestimates the mythological culture of that age and the fact that e.g. the whole nation of Israel was based on a foundation of mythology (the Exodus story).

In his magisterial volume *The Resurrection of the Son of God* Wright explains how he believed the resurrection occurred. He maintains that there was a 'transphysical event', a 'transforming revivication' of the dead body of Jesus, accounted for historically by the empty tomb and the meetings, denying that any other explanation is empirically possible.[26]

However, we have to say, that such a firm rebuttal of other

---

[25] *The Resurrection of Jesus, The Crossan-Wright Debate.* SPCK. London. 2006. p38.
[26] Ibid. chs. 14–19. p616ff.

possible explanations is quite unjustified and denies the work of other significant theologians, which, in itself, is quite unprofessional.

Hellen Giblin-Jowett (19**)

Hellen is a young literary scholar and feminist theologian living in Newcastle upon Tyne. In an email to this author (12.12.20) she expresses her views, "For me the resurrection is to be understood as a question of texts generating other texts, so I'd slot the resurrection story alongside other dying and rising god mythologies. Paola Corente, a Peruvian professor, concludes that the resurrection story is ubiquitous among humans and that the Christian tradition does not have an exclusive monopoly on it. I think that within the narrative the most important thing about Jesus' dying is that his dead physical body left us with the Holy Ghost (Spirit). Although it is an important opportunity to articulate grief, the traditional concentration on the actual corporeal composition of Christ is misguided and pointless because the biblical story straightway heads off to the Upper Room. To me that's the point of the empty tomb – Jesus is gone now so it's up to us. Just like the Cenotaph in Whitehall, it's an invitation to us to come on in as individuals and fill it up imaginatively with our own unique psychohistories."

Daniel A. Smith (19**)

He is currently Assistant Professor of New Testament Language and Literature at Huron University College, London, Ontario, Canada. In an interesting perspective on the resurrection he says, "Mark has told the story in which Jesus was raised in such a way that there is no question that the body is absent from the tomb. Jesus is dead and gone but has also been raised by God. According to Mark, then, the crucified One has been taken away into heaven and raised by God, and is now there in a bodily way (just as Elijah and Moses and one supposes Enoch as well) waiting to reappear as Son of Man."[27] So Smith is suggesting that the Assumption and Resurrection traditions have been combined in such a way that the Easter story will be further developed by Luke, Matthew and John with accounts of bodily appearances. This is a revival of Old Testament mythology which would appeal to a Jewish audience but strains modern credibility.

Conclusion.

This concludes our brief survey of a representative group of scholars illustrating the wide range of thinking with regard to the resurrection, from that of a literal physical, historic event through to its rejection in that form, and onto the view of it being symbolic in nature. It appears that you 'pays your money and you takes your choice!' Nevertheless, there is help from among them as we continue our search for what really happened and what it means.

---

[27] David A. Smith. *Revisiting the Empty Tomb: The Early History of Easter.* Fortress Press. 2010. p97.

Chapter 11
What Actually Happened?

a) Scientific Explanations.

Those who argue for a literal, physical, historic resurrection often say that God made use of certain natural laws, known only to Him, in raising the body of Jesus back to life. (e.g. see N.T. Wright *The Resurrection of the Son of God* in chapter 10 and his ideas of a trans-physical event).

It is argued, for instance, that Einstein's theory of relativity rendered Newton's Laws of Motion obsolete, therefore there may be, as yet, laws undiscovered by scientists, used by God to perform the miracle of the resurrection, just as Newton's laws no longer apply under specific conditions found deep in outer space. Therefore, it is said, the laws of nature may not strictly apply in the case of the resurrection as the conditions may be uniquely different from normal.

However, it is quite unlikely that such would be the case on that particular Easter Sunday morning in Palestine.

Quantum theory is also sometimes cited in support of the possibility of Christ's resurrection, energy being made up of 'quanta' which behave like particles or waves and do not necessarily conform to conventional patterns as illustrated by Schrodinger's cat which is placed in a closed box with a capsule of cyanide. It is never known whether the capsule is broken, therefore the cat may be both dead and alive at one and the same time. The real situation can only be discovered by breaking open the box. This gives rise to the multi-universe theory that parallel universes exist which equal the number of states an object may exist in at any one time. It is therefore a (crazy?) conclusion to draw that Jesus may be both dead and alive at one and the same time, alive in our universe but dead in another.

N.T. Wright believes that concerning the resurrection of Jesus Christ, a 'trans-physical' event may have occurred perhaps involving quantum physics. However, there is no reason to believe that, at the time, normal conditions did not appertain. It is dishonest to 'bend' science in order to prove the unproveable, the impossible and any preconceived ideas. For instance, this author once had a book sent to him containing 'scientific' proof that the earth was created in seven days in the year 4004BC. A creationist museum in the USA is based on this hypothesis. The abuse of scripture in opposition to proven scientific facts or strongly verified theories lacks intellectual integrity.

Chaos theory is also cited as being in support of the physical, historic resurrection of Jesus. States of disorder, randomness or irregularity are nevertheless governed by determinative patterns, for instance butterfly wings flapping in the UK could be the cause of a hurricane in China. Small differences in initial conditions may yield wildly diverging outcomes. If chaos is the breakdown of asymmetry then that only opens up an infinitesimally small possibility of a resurrection occurring.

String theory states that the fundamental constituents of the universe are one-dimensional strings of particles rather than single entities. It describes the interaction of particles which are actually vibrations shaped like loops of string each with its own frequency, creating extra dimensions of space within gravity fields, thus open to the possibility of an unusual occurrence such as a resurrection.

The Occum's Razor principle states that where two explanations account for all the facts the simpler one is more likely to be correct. Therefore, the simpler explanation for the empty tomb is that the body has been removed. But the use of Occum's razor could also unjustifiably discount more than two complicated explanations which may probably be true. The subject of the resurrection is much more complex than such an either/or situation. There are many complex psychological factors to take into account as well as dispute about basic facts. As C.F. Evans writes:

"It is an extraordinary but indisputable fact that the four Gospels diverge from one another so widely in both their beginnings and their endings. The best explanation of this now seems to be that the evangelists did not understand themselves primarily as reporters of events, but as tellers of stories through which the gospel can be heard."[28]

The brief outline of the above theories is very much that of a lay person's understanding, which is usually baffled by a world of physics way beyond comprehension. In each case a resurrection becomes possible, but this would still require

---

[28] C.F. Evans in *A dictionary of Biblical Interpretation,* SCM London. 1990, Eds. R.J.C0ggins & J.L. Houlden, p587.

God to be an interventionist which, as we have seen in Chapter 9, He is not. The explanation as to what actually happened on Easter day itself lies elsewhere.

b) What Actually Happened?

There was a period of about seven weeks between the Passover and the death and entombment of Jesus and the events of the Day of Pentecost according to the New Testament stories. How did the disciples spend that time? We have only sketchy information but it is fairly safe to assume that it was spent in a way that, from our own experience, grieving people usually do, spending time with family and associates and visiting people and places connected with Jesus and reliving memories. There are clues in the stories which suggest they did just that. For instance:

1. They regularly assembled together in the Upper Room. (Luke 24.33–49; John 20.19–23; John 20.24–29; Acts 2.1).
2. They continued their Temple worship. (Luke 24.52–53).
3. One of them visited the garden where, possibly, she had met Jesus previously. (John 20.11–18).
4. Some of them walked the road to Emmaus which they had probably previously travelled with Jesus, culminating in a meal with Cleopas and a friend. (Luke 24.13–32).
5. Others visited Bethany for a meal, possibly at the home of Mary, Martha and Lazarus, and where nearby, Jesus apparently, also gave them a blessing.

(Luke 24.50–51).

6.   Some of them travelled back to Galilee where they went on a fishing trip (John 21.1–14, cf. Luke 5.1–11), and recalled previous conversations (John 21.15–19; John 21.20–24).

7.   And whilst in Galilee, they visited a mountain special to them, possibly Hermon, the Mount of the Transfiguration and from where Jesus was said, later, to have 'ascended' after their 'commissioning' (Matthew 28.16–20).

8.   Finally, they had all obviously arranged to meet together in the upper room to celebrate the Feast of Pentecost as devout Jews would do (Acts 2.1ff).

In each and every place they would have a strong sense of the presence of the One whose life and ministry they had shared for the space of about three years, and from whom tragic events had parted. The resurrection appearance stories of Jesus correspond to experiences which would normally be expected of grieving loved ones.

At the end of their seven weeks of grieving and coming to terms with the inestimable enormity of their loss, i.e. their long and greatly expected 'Messiah' was dead and gone, the disciples possibly plus a few others, met, as previously arranged, in the Upper Room to celebrate the Feast of Pentecost, being of 'one accord in one place' (Acts 2.1).

Now was the peak of their corporate grieving to be realised in an experience so intense that they came to a sublime consciousness that what Christ had incarnated in his life and work and teaching would last forever. It was a moment of sheer enlightenment. It was if a bunch of

'Damascus Road' type encounters happened all at once, a group experience in which they felt an undeniable presence of overwhelming power, and an ecstatic, motivating, inspirational, will-changing event with immediate consequences. They descended to the street below and began to share their good news with palpable excitement, such that bystanders remarked upon their 'intoxicated' state (v.13).

The symbolism in the story; wind, fire, ecstatic speech, is redolent of Old testament imagery, a reversal of Babel and a reminder of Moses at the burning bush when the deliverance of the Hebrew people from their slavery began. The cosmopolitan crowd evidently, to a large extent, seemed to view the Pentecost event as of being of divine activity (vs. 11), enough to prompt them to ask, "What does this mean?" to which Peter's sermon gave the answer (vs. 14ff) So it was that the 'Day of Pentecost' event became the occasion on which, "Christ is Risen" became the foundational incident which gave birth to the Church.

Naturally all of this sanctified speculation is impossible of any historical proof but with a great deal of probability because what the disciples did matches with our own grief experiences as they arrived at their own moment of resolution. This theorising is no more and no less valid than that of the existing stories in the Gospels, believed to have been recorded from memory mixed with a great deal of imagination, but obviously somewhat incredulous.

The Day of Pentecost is thus a key event in our understanding of the resurrection of Jesus. Those seven weeks of grief-stricken activity came to an end with their gathering together and a build-up of emotions to this epoch-making climax.

What really happened on that significant day we do not know and can never know, except that something did, unless a brilliant scientist invents a time machine and makes H. G. Wells' futuristic novel become a reality. By all accounts, it must have been a spiritually, psychologically, transformative, consciousness changing group experience which produced a profound conviction that the Jesus who was definitely and conclusively dead, nevertheless was 'alive' and 'let loose in the world' as his Other Self the Holy Spirit.

Whether this was all the product of human psychological processes or a matter of divine intervention is open for debate. The event itself certainly set in train an historical series of activities leading to the Church as Christ's continuing incarnation, or as Bonhoeffer puts it 'Christ existing as Community'. What must be regarded as the 'power of mystery' created an ongoing phenomenon, which, mainly for good, but sometimes unfortunately for ill has had a profound influence upon the history of humankind.

But it may be asked, if the resurrection was a corporate vision like that of St Paul on the Damascus Road but for a group rather than an individual, how could it be said to have been a real resurrection experience? It was real in that it was an experience apprehended by the senses of those present in the upper room. Whatever was felt and seen on the occasion of the Day of Pentecost created a deeply held conviction that death had not defeated the purpose for which Christ came into the world and that somehow he lived on as an objectively substantial presence with the disciples and also with their successors, both individually and corporately ever since, as experienced and celebrated in their fellowship gatherings and the Eucharist. It is a sense of this reality which sustains the true body of believers in their worship and witness in the world. As indeed the early Methodists expressed it so well:

"What we have felt and seen,

with confidence we tell,

and publish to the sons of men,

the signs infallible."[29]

Thus as the depths of their grief changed into the euphoric heights of their conscious realisation that death had not had the last word so far as Jesus was concerned, the disciples, now renamed apostles, felt so convinced of the of the truth of resurrection in this manner that it became a significant element in their preaching, and as was shown by C. H. Dodd a generation or so ago[30], an essential part of their *kerygma* the core of the message which they proclaimed wherever they travelled in order to establish churches. We now have to ask, "What was the content of the resurrection message which they proclaimed far and wide?"

---

[29] Charles Wesley, *Methodist Hymn Book* no.377 vs.2

[30] In his *The Apostolic Preaching and its Developments.*

Chapter 12
The Kerygma Enigma

It is often affirmed that the resurrection of Jesus Christ is at the very heart of the Christian Faith and indeed the foundation of it, but it is also one of its greatest stumbling blocks insofar as credibility is concerned. Nevertheless, the resurrection, or the preaching of it, formed part of the *kerygma*, the core message, of the early Church, preached far and wide by the itinerant apostles, notably Paul, arising out of his Damascene experience. The principal mentions in the Acts of the Apostles of preaching events are: in Jerusalem (2:24,32) (3.15) (4.10,33) (5.30,42); in Samaria (8.25); Ashdod and Caesarea (8.40); Athens (17.31ff) etc.

The question is, what was the nature of the resurrection message taken by the apostles across the Mediterranean world and elsewhere in their missionary endeavours? It was probably the Jewish understanding of 'resurrection' at that time because the infant Church had not yet grown out of the cultural and theological influences of its cradle religion.

During a considerable part of the Old Testament it was the Jewish belief that the dead entered Sheol which was conceived as a shadowy underworld sort of place from which God was absent.

However other views did develop. Daniel 12.2 speaks of the resurrection of both the righteous and the wicked who would all appear for judgement before the 'Son of Man'. The inter-testament period saw a growth in apocalyptic and the belief that God would vindicate the faithful and judge between the righteous and the wicked. There would be a dramatic coming to earth of a triumphant Messianic figure before whom all would be judged.

Exceptionally, however, the party of the Sadducees argued that the resurrection of the dead could not be proven from the Pentateuch (Torah) and so disbelieved in it.

As we know apocalyptic ideas were attached to Jesus and were continued on into the early Church and for a time formed part of its message, a clear example being 1 Thess. 4.13–5.11. After some years had elapsed however, it began to be realised that the 'risen and ascended Christ', thought to be seated at the 'right hand of God', was not going to float down from the skies and exercise a general judgement of humankind, but for a while the preaching of the gospel, including a mention of resurrection, must have also included such apocalyptic elements. It is not surprising therefore that the Greek intelligentsia ridiculed them (Acts 17.30–32 in Athens). The idea of a general resurrection to judge the 'quick and the dead' was quite unacceptable to them. Although they had a post mortem mythology of their own they hesitated to accept the Jewish/Christian notion of the resurrection of the body, as indeed we would do so today, science consigning such mythology to the realm of historical curiosities.

Chapter 13
Vision and Veracity

This writer had a practising Methodist as his religious education teacher (a Mr A. Pearson Jones) at the Doncaster Technical High School for Boys in the 1950s. In approaching the more unusual Bible stories, he taught that we should always seek a rational explanation. Moses at the 'burning bush' for example, may be explained as a prolifically flowering shrub through which bright sunlight shone to give the impression of a fiery presence symbolising the numinosity of divine being. A similar experience accompanies the sun shining on a flowering forsythia in full bloom in the author's garden.

It is not difficult to bring imagination to the visionary experience of the Day of Pentecost in that crowded upper room. It would be a bright and sunny Palestinian day with perhaps strong cool breezes blowing in through the open windows, quite likely at that time of year, lending the suggestion of 'fire and wind' symbolising the Holy Spirit. A highly charged emotional atmosphere would be ready to sense the powerful presence of the one for whom they had deeply grieved for the space of those seven weeks. As 'living' and 'risen' he was about to be known to be with them. Again, as with Paul on the Damascus Road, this was to be a truly transformative encounter for the disciples, one which motivated them for their effective missionary task across the Roman world. Such a view as this fits all the facts as we find them in the New Testament and also accords with our own real-life grieving experiences.

There is no doubt that life-changing visionary events are part of the ongoing spiritual experiences of God's people. Stories abound in the Bible of such transforming occasions, Jacob's wrestling, Moses at the burning bush, Isaiah in the Temple, Ezekiel's wheels within wheels, Daniel's vision of the 'son of man', and on from the Old Testament into the New, the story of the Transfiguration of Jesus, Peter's vision of a great sheet containing living creatures, Paul on the Damascus Road and so on.

The prophet Joel seems to expect that the result of the outpouring of the Holy Spirit will be that, "Your old men will have dreams and your young men will see visions." (ch.2.28)

With regard to the Pentecost Day experience, it is contended that the disciples, as fit and healthy young men in the upper room, had a corporate visionary experience of Jesus Christ such that they were able to declare, "He is Risen."

Edward S. Ames defines visions as, "Mental states in which the subject seems to see objects and persons with lifelike clearness though others present have no such experience."[31]

Another definition of a vision is that of E. C. Blackman, "An ecstatic experience in which new knowledge is revealed

---

[31] E.S. Ames in eds. S. Matthews & G.B. Smith, *A Dictionary of Religion and Ethics.* Waverley. London. 1921. p468

through something seen."[32]

With regard to such stories in the Bible, (both O.T. and N.T.) readers before comparatively modern times would not be concerned to distinguish between a reported vision as, "A literary device or an event that took place in real time and physical space, nor would they have made a sharp distinction between a vision, which is essentially an internal experience, and an observation, seeing actual figures in front of their eyes."[33]

There is no doubt that such visions are real for those who experience them, even though they may take place in the mind, and are often, if not usually, experienced by the individual, although instances of corporate visionary experiences are reputed to have occurred also.

So far as the individual is concerned they seem to happen when certain physical and psychological conditions appertain, for instance, during periods of extreme tiredness, following a time of fasting or self-denial of some kind, or under pressure of personal events such as a bereavement or a great loss of some nature, or at any time when the mind is not behaving normally for some accountable reason, or occasions when the very *raison d'être* of an individual is called into question at the deepest level of personality, such as that of Paul on the Damascus Road, who at the time was suffering from a suppressed complex.

It is not uncommon for visions to occur in the teenage

---

[32] E.C. Blackman in ed. A. Richardson, *A Theological Word Book of the Bible,* SCM. London, 1957 edn. p277

[33] J.C. Adams, *From Literal to Literary,* Rising Star Press. Oregan. 2005. p265

years when emotions are susceptible to feelings of guilt, often induced in hot-house evangelical atmospheres when pressures to become 'converted' are applied. Such an experience happened to this author following the visit of a charismatic evangelical teacher to a youth fellowship. There are numerous accounts of people who have 'seen' Jesus in the privacy of their own rooms not least one known to this writer when the wife of a Methodist Local Preacher testified to such an appearance in her own bedroom which her husband was prepared to believe even though he had not seen!

But insofar as visions are concerned, psychology cannot account for all the factors at work. Many influences come into play, consciously and subconsciously, from both past and present life experiences.

A further definition is afforded by Wikipedia:

"A vision is something seen in a dream, trance or religious ecstasy, especially a supernatural appearance that usually conveys a revelation."[34]

Neurotheology is a discipline which attempts to explain religious experience and behaviour in neuro-scientific terms:

"It is the study of correlations of neural phenomena with subjective experiences of spirituality and hypotheses to explain these phenomena... proponents of the neuroscience of religion say that there is a neurological and evolutionary basis for subjective experiences traditionally categorised as spiritual or religious."[35]

Of course, to explain such experiences does not mean that they are neither true nor real, and we may conclude that the

---

[34] Wikipedia website.
[35] Ibid.

states of mind and emotions on the Day of Pentecost as the disciples met together, were such that a momentous vision of some kind was possible, and, as it happened, did occur.

If the stories of the resurrection appearances of Jesus are, as we have argued, grief stories, then the experience on the Day of Pentecost is the single authentic corporate visionary experience of the "Risen Christ", the meaning of which is explored and expressed in literary form by signs, symbols and metaphors.

Chapter 14
Signs, Symbols and Metaphors

God has given us a book full of stories,
which was made for His people of old,
it begins with the tale of a garden,
and ends with the city of gold.[36]

This simple verse from a Victorian children's hymn is more profound than appears at first sight. The era of critical scholarship with regard to the Bible has gradually given us to understand that it is indeed a book full of stories, rather than verifiable historical narratives. In fact, we may go as far as to say that very little, if anything, in the Bible is literal provable history consisting as it does of story, poetry, didactics, apocalyptic fantasy and other kinds of literature.

Whether or not some of the story passages were intended to be a historic record we do not know nor ever will. The people, in biblical times, lived according to their stories, which, in the first place, were orally transmitted. These were their foundation myths, as we may say, especially the stories of the patriarchs, the exodus and the return, as well as the

---

[36] *Methodist Hymn Book,* 1933. No. 857, by Maria Matilda Penstone, 1859–1910.

vivid imagery of apocalyptic which gave them hope for the future when times were hard.

Behind the literary format of passages of scripture lies the sense of intangible meanings and unexpressed faith and beliefs. It has been left to us to define these by our various interpretations and theologies constructed from the raw material of the texts themselves with not a little philosophical enterprise. And so we are led to consider the place of sign, symbol and metaphor as related to the resurrection appearance stories. With the help of the O.E.D. we may define these terms.

Sign: An act of a miraculous nature serving to demonstrate divine power or authority.

Symbol: Something that stands for, represents, or denotes something else, especially a material object representing or taken to represent something immaterial or abstract.

Metaphor: The figure of speech in which a name or a descriptive term is transferred to some object to which it is not properly applicable.

The story of the resurrection is a SIGN pointing beyond itself to that of a greater reality, the truth that life emerges from death as evidenced in the world of nature and human existence, the seeds of new life produced by the processes of change and decay. In the created world, life will flourish even in the most threatening of circumstances. Polluted industrial sites, even radioactive ones, if left to nature, will green themselves. Blades of grass are seen even to crack concrete given time and a flaw in the cement. In nature, the processes of life emerging from death is a regular phenomenon and in the animal world the predatory pattern prevails in that for life to continue it must feed on life, the death of creatures in the lower orders crucial to the continuance of life in the higher. The annual miracle of springtime, nature's very own resurrection, occurs without fail.

In the Bible, SIGNS have a long pedigree. The people would look for a 'sign' to authenticate a prophet's message or to confirm that a certain course of action was 'of God'. The prophets would perform 'acted parables' to give a visual substance to their message. In the Gospels, on occasion, the critics of Jesus would demand a sign of him as proof of his alleged divine identity. He refused to perform a sign to prove anything, when, as he affirmed, his life, work and teaching should speak for themselves. If he did, then this would also be a contradiction of the repudiation by Jesus in his temptations of the rejection of the use of signs and wonders to extend the Kingdom of God. Would he ever have agreed therefore to the sign of a resurrection to prove his identity? Or is the resurrection a later idea conceived by the early Church to furnish proof of Christ's status as an incarnation of the divine? However that may be, the healing miracle stories are signs, to the Gospel writer, of the breaking through into this world of the eternal life of the Kingdom of God.

The story of the resurrection is a SYMBOL of the new life which emerges from the old when a person begins a faith commitment to Jesus Christ, following him as a disciple and entering upon the life of the Kingdom of God, "If anyone is in Christ, he is a new creation."[37]

Symbols, also, in the Bible, have an important significance, examples being the symbol of the rainbow given as the assurance of a flood free world in future, of the snake

---

[37] 2. Corinthians 5.17

raised on a pole in the wilderness, sight of which was to heal the people. The golden calf was created as an anti-god symbol by a rebellious people. The altars of the patriarchs were constructed as meeting places between God and themselves. The Temple was constructed as a symbol of the universal power and presence of God and its content was full of symbolic artefacts conveying meanings of the elements of the peoples' worship.

The symbols of the empty tomb and a corpse-less cross speak of powerful theological themes such as the victory of life over death, love over hatred, hope over despair, truth over falsehood, right over wrong, light over darkness, forgiveness over revenge and retribution, justice over injustice, all of which are positive moral and spiritual victories, particularly the triumph of good over evil. The world would indeed be lost if the latter were not true, that, on balance, in any given circumstances, goodness does ultimately have the edge over evil.

Worth pondering over!

"The American poet Wallace Stephens said that we do not live in the world, but in a picture of it, voicing a radical apprehension of the symbolic nature of all thinking and doing whereby we get to grips with the world."[38] We may infer from this that there is very little, that is not in any way symbolic, presumably the opposite of symbol being fact itself.

The story of the resurrection is a METAPHOR for that hope which springs eternal in the human spirit in that something new and creative and better is always a possibility.

---

[38] Eds. R.J. Coggins & J.L. Houlden, *A Dictionary of Religion and Ethics.* SCM. London. 1990. P655, under *'Symbol'* by J. Drury.

No matter how dire and dark any situation is the hope of something transformationally different emerging from it is an ever-present factor.

Examples of metaphor in the Bible may also be cited, e.g. phrases such as 'The Servant', 'The Body of Christ', 'The New Jerusalem', etc., the "I am's" of John's Gospel being supreme; Christ as 'The Door', 'The Bread of Life', 'The Light of the World', 'The Vine', etc, with the 'I am the Resurrection and the Life' being the most significant of these. However, the story of the raising of Lazarus arose and what really happened will never be known, except to say that it is recorded to express the view that Jesus as 'Son of God' must have had extraordinary powers, even so great as doing the impossible – raising the dead. Here again there is a contradiction with the Temptation experience and the rejection by Jesus of the concept of his becoming a wonder working Messiah.

The Lazarus story arose out of a prior conviction regarding the nature of Jesus as somebody especially divine, and could not realistically have been a real event in time.

In conclusion, with regard to the resurrection we have but one fact which serves as a sign, symbol and metaphor, that is the empty tomb, the sight of which gave rise to the conclusion that something unusual had taken place, i.e., that Jesus was bodily raised from the tomb, an assumption which gave rise to the appearance stories and subsequently to various metaphysical interpretations (see chapter 10). So in a rather complex whirlpool of interpretations, the resurrection of Jesus is sign, symbol and metaphor all at one and the same time, but nevertheless which is an indication of a reality of a spiritual and eternal nature, a reality beyond words which impinges upon human experience for those who have living faith.

But was the resurrection, as is claimed, the foundation event which began the existence of the early Church as a movement? Not if it was not part of the original message of Jesus himself as he began his work in the world. His Gospel (good news), in the first instance, contained no reference to his resurrection, whether hinted at or firmly predicted.

Chapter 15
The Real Gospel

Concentration upon such subjects as birth and resurrection stories, celebrating such events and wasting ink 'proving' them, not to mention theories of the atonement, the second coming, biblical inspiration, the place of popes, bishops, priests and deacons, is all a massive distraction from the essential message of Jesus which concerns the Kingdom of God, the announcement of its imminence, how it may be entered and the practical out workings which it entails as expressed in his teachings.

In fact, we could go so far as to say that the substantial attention given to 'supernatural' phenomena supposedly associated with Jesus is 'demonic', because it means that thought is not given as fully as it should be to issues such as love, justice, righteousness, freedom and peace, which have to do with faithful discipleship and obedience to the teaching of Jesus. These are the issues that Christians should have at the forefront of their minds not arguments about what happened in stables and tombs long, long ago.

Jesus' mission was to introduce us all to the Kingdom of God which very much relates to this life and leaves any after death life as a matter of speculation and unlikely to be proven as a fact. We each have the gift of this one earthly life and we are called to use it responsibly as servants of one another in love of God and of neighbour as ourselves.

"The resurrection is everything, if there's no resurrection we're done," said a fellow Methodist minister to me in a conversation recently. I beg to differ. Jesus did not say, "This is the good news, I was born of a virgin and I will rise from the dead."

The stories of the virgin birth and the resurrection arose because of a desire to assert that Jesus was someone special, even divine, and to demonstrate the superiority of Christianity over other forms of mystical religions, especially those of Greece and Rome, with their similar stories and unwarranted claims to supernatural origins.

Moreover, if Jesus was raised then that could be said to be a denial of the doctrine of the incarnation. If Jesus, 'Son of God', truly became human then he must be subject to death as an absolute finality just like the rest of us. Again, if Jesus was raised then God is monstrously unjust. Why should He raise one particular man and treat him as special and not raise others who have also suffered cruel and unfair torture and death, not to mention, come to the rescue of millions of people who are refugees, starving, captive to disease, oppressed and victims of war and natural disaster.

Also, it has been taught and believed for generations that the resurrection is the one foundation stone of the Christian faith, that through this one event a life of eternity has been made possible for humankind, especially, exclusively, for those who are 'believers'. In my view, the essence of Christianity is the message of Jesus, as substantiated by his life and ministry, a message that has to do with the here and now of our life in the world. Mark, the first Gospel to be written, has no account of any birth or of any resurrection it simply presents the challenge of the new way of life which Jesus offers, a life of faithful discipleship with the costly risks of personal sacrifice, which, as was the case with him, has the possibility of death.

a) The Good News of the Kingdom of God

Jesus said, "The right time has come, the Kingdom of God is near, repent (change your minds) and believe the good news." (Mark 1.15)

According to C.H. Dodd in his important seminal work, *The Parables of the Kingdom*[39] the parables of Jesus are all about nothing more and nothing less than the Kingdom of God itself. This is the sole import of his teaching and his stories, taken from real life, help to illustrate the nature of that Kingdom (or Realm) of God. Indeed, the rest of his recorded teaching is about the ethics of the Kingdom, that is the behaviour of those who belong to it, both between themselves and towards others, fellow human beings, neighbours and even enemies.

But we need to ask what is the Kingdom of God and what did Jesus mean by it? It is a phrase with a long history. The Jews believed that, from the time of Abraham onwards they were a special people chosen by God. They occupied a so-called 'Promised land' and appointed a king. There grew up a dream among them that one day Israel would rule the nations with Jerusalem as the capital of the world and that they would lead people everywhere into a realm of justice and peace. But

---

[39] Revised edition, Fontana, 1961

this dream was shattered by a series of events.

1. The division of the kingdom into two parts, North and South, following Solomon's death in 900BC.
2. The destruction of the Northern Kingdom in 725BC by the Assyrians.
3. The conquest of the Southern Kingdom in 585BC by the Babylonians and the deportation of the people.
4. After their return to their own country and the start of the rebuilding of Jerusalem in 440BC and then the reign of the Maccabees they were conquered again by the Greeks and then by the Romans who, as we know, ruled in Judea in the time of Jesus.

Throughout all these circumstances the dream of the Kingdom of God never died. As a small oppressed nation, the people believed that one day God would intervene and, at a stroke, make things right for them, their enemies would be destroyed and they would be supreme and rule the nations. A powerful Messiah would appear on the scene and make it all happen and lead them into this triumphant new age.

But then Jesus came along and put a spoke in the wheel! He said that it would not be like that at all. The Kingdom of God is not about political power or raising an army to build an empire. The Kingdom of God is a realm in which the love of God rules and which is based on the ideals of forgiveness and justice, freedom and peace, and the loving self-sacrificial service of others, being a Kingdom not wholly of this world.

Jesus came to change people's perceptions and to give them a vision of a world society in which everyone has equal status and where those in most need are given priority. And so the Kingdom of God is an entity which is radically different from anything the world has ever known before. It is found everywhere that God's love rules and where people are obedient to the demands of that love. Jesus goes on to say how we may enter the Kingdom. We have to undergo a process of repentance, a change of heart and mind in which the new focus of our lives is to live the life of that Kingdom. It takes a deliberate act of the will and it means forsaking the values of the world in which we live with all its materialism and consumerism, its celebrity worship and self-concern and embracing the ideals of love, love of God and neighbour as oneself, entering upon a life of sacrificial service one toward another, prioritising the marginalised and neglected of society, the left behind people and the forgotten people, people oppressed by uncompassionate systems.

Thus in joining the Kingdom we live to practise its values as expressed in the Kingdom stories to be found in the Gospels. For instance, the parable of the unforgiving servant (Matthew 18.21–35) emphasises that forgiveness is the foundation stone of the Kingdom of God. Forgiveness is not calculated and has no limits. It is not conditional, except that those who are forgiven are expected to forgive. Forgiveness is of God to whom we pray to be forgiven as we forgive those who sin against us. Forgiveness is a powerful force for healing as seen, for example, in the work of the Commission for Truth and reconciliation in South Africa. Archbishop Desmond Tutu has also taken part in extending the process into Northern Ireland. On a personal level, forgiveness is the way in which relationships are healed and maintained through openness and trust.

The story of the owner/workers in the vineyard (Matthew

20.1–16) is about the justice of God and the fair treatment of people one toward another. Different workers are hired at different times of the day and work for different hours yet are all paid the same. A trade unionist's nightmare! But the story is about the generosity of the owner towards those most in need, workers – people who were perhaps not so able as the others and could only work for less time, but they had hungry and needy families too. The justice of the kingdom always ensures that each one has enough. From each according to his ability to each according to their need means that social implications follow on from our convictions about the nature of the Kingdom of God.

The story of the Good Samaritan (Luke 10.25–37) goes even further by showing that as far as human need is concerned the issues of race and religion are irrelevant. Jesus tells the parable in answer to a scribe's question, "Who is my neighbour?" The Samaritan, by giving help to the injured Jew thinks nothing of the deep differences between them as far as race and religion are concerned which barriers are as nothing in the face of human need. The story has much to say to today's multi-faith society. In the last analysis, what people believe takes second place to their needs.

The parable of the sheep and the goats (Matthew 25.31–46) again underlines this point. It is those who fed the hungry, gave drink to the thirsty, welcomed the stranger, clothed the naked and visited the prisoner who inherited the Kingdom and served their Christ. Doing those things to the least of people meant that they were doing them as unto Him, albeit unknowingly.

Such is the nature of the Kingdom of God as described by Jesus in the Gospels, the good news being that it is here and waiting for humanity to enter into it.

b) Jesus' Manifesto for Ministry and Mission

Jesus also said, "The Spirit of the Lord is upon me because he has chosen me to bring good news to the poor. He has sent me to proclaim liberty to the captives and recovery of sight to the blind, to set free the oppressed to and announce that the time has come when the Lord will save His people." (Luke 4.18–19)

Was Jesus a politician? He was not a far right-wing Herodian nor an extreme left-wing Zealot, but he did encourage political action of a kind, like go the second mile or give away both coat and shirt to Roman soldiers! He said, "Love your enemies." Beginning in Nazareth, he took the pattern of his ministry from Isaiah the prophet, the direct opposite of Messianic expectation. He came to bring:

1. **Good News to the poor**: The poor are always with you, said Jesus, but not as an inevitable fact. They want to hear the good news that their poverty is history. Matthew wrote, "Blessed are the poor in spirit," whereas Luke said, "Blessed are the poor – who are in the Kingdom of God NOW," meaning that we are to struggle for justice alongside them by doing what we can to support agencies which help the poor and by helping to shape political opinion in their favour.

2. **Liberty for the captives:** Far too many people are held captive because they fight for freedom and justice, as Nelson Mandela was. Today, Amnesty

campaigns to set captives free. Slavery still exists in various forms today, migrants work for a pittance, women and girls are forced into prostitution, sweatshop workers produce goods cheaply. Both John the Baptist and Jesus were unjustly imprisoned and executed. They shared the plight of the captives whom Jesus desires to be free.

3. **Recovery of sight for the blind:** This is a difficult phrase! Whatever you think about the miracle stories, some of them tell us that Jesus helped the blind to see and he exercised a healing ministry with his caring touch. Helping the 'blind' to see is the work of certain groups today. But does this phrase mean more than just physical blindness? Those who are the cause of poverty, exploitation and oppression need to 'see' the evil they are responsible for and to correct the injustices they perpetrate.

4. **Freedom for the Oppressed:** The Jews knew all about oppression. The Romans were good at it. They imposed heavy taxes to keep the Empire going. Any sign of trouble was ruthlessly suppressed. Human rights are on the world's agenda today. People everywhere both expect and demand their freedom. But there are still dictators and oppressive regimes. Activists struggle at great personal cost to gain hard won freedoms. There is economic oppression too. Every human being is created in the divine image and has a right to enjoy true freedom with responsibility.

5. **Announcing Salvation:** Salvation means different things to different people, but in the time of Jesus it meant deliverance from the Romans by a powerful

Messiah. Jesus however denied such limited nationalism. For him salvation had to do with the coming of the Kingdom of God and the wholeness of life in every aspect. The challenge of Jesus to all of us is to change our hearts and minds and live the life of the Kingdom, based on love, justice, freedom and peace, all of which are inter-related.

Jesus was born for a purpose. He took his manifesto for ministry straight from Isaiah 61. In his first sermon in the synagogue at Nazareth he presented his programme designed to elevate the whole of human life. It could be adopted by every church as a mission statement to bring good news to the poor, liberty to the captives, to open eyes closed to the needs of others, to set free the oppressed, to announce God's work of salvation, and to do those things with every means at our disposal. The proof that the Spirit of the Lord is upon the Church, as it was upon Jesus, is to see God's people doing these things in the world today. For his manifesto is that of his disciples also. This is the Good News; the real Gospel.